Innovations in Education Series
Edited by Robert J. Brown

1. Edward J. Dirkswager, editor. *Teachers as Owners: A Key to Revitalizing Public Education.* 2002.

2. Darlene Leiding. *The Won't Learners: An Answer to Their Cry.* 2002.

3. Ronald J. Newell. *Passion for Learning: How a Project-Based System Meets the Needs of High School Students in the 21st Century.* 2003.

4. Sarah J. Noonan. *The Elements of Leadership: What You Should Know.* 2003.

5. Jeffrey R. Cornwall. *From the Ground Up: Entrepreneurial School Leadership.* 2003.

From the Ground Up

Entrepreneurial School Leadership

Jeffrey R. Cornwall

A SCARECROWEDUCATION BOOK

The Scarecrow Press, Inc.
Lanham, Maryland, and Oxford
2003

A SCARECROWEDUCATION BOOK

Published in the United States of America
by Scarecrow Press, Inc.
A wholly owned subsidiary of the Rowman & Littlefield Publishing Group, Inc.
4501 Forbes Boulevard, Suite 200, Lanham, Maryland 20706
www.scarecroweducation.com

P.O. Box 317
Oxford
OX2 9RU, UK

British Library Cataloguing in Publication Information Available

Library of Congress Cataloging-in-Publication Data

Cornwall, Jeffrey R.
 From the ground up : entrepreneurial school leadership / Jeffrey R.
Cornwall.
    p. cm. — (Innovations in education)
 "A ScarecrowEducation book."
 Includes bibliographical references (p.   ) and index.
 ISBN 1-57886-020-2 (pbk. : alk. paper)
  1. Educational leadership—United States. 2. Entrepreneurship—United
States. I. Title. II. Series: Innovations in education (Lanham, Md.)
LB2805 .C6593 2003
371.2—dc21
                                                                    2003005519

♾™ The paper used in this publication meets the minimum requirements of
American National Standard for Information Sciences—Permanence of
Paper for Printed Library Materials, ANSI/NISO Z39.48-1992.
Manufactured in the United States of America.

119718

Contents

Acknowledgments

I would like to thank Dr. Robert Brown, who provided insight and guidance throughout the development of this book. Thanks as well to Katie Thayer for her work in conducting interviews used in the book. Thanks to the educational entrepreneurs, including Ramona Rosales, Dr. Karen Rusthoven, and Mathew Metz, who provided insightful and honest stories on their efforts to turn their visions into successful schools. And once again, I cannot possible thank Betsy Lofgren enough for her thoughtful editing and support. Entrepreneurs like my father, Robert Cornwall, and educators like my father-in-law, Robert Spanbauer, inspired this book. Finally, thanks to my wife, Ann, for her confidence, encouragement, and partnership throughout all my careers and adventures.

PART 1

The Idea Phase

CHAPTER 1

Introduction

The landscape of K–12 education across the United States is changing dramatically. While still the dominant choice of most families, enrollment in traditional public schools is predicted to remain fairly constant through 2010. Enrollment in public schools reached a plateau of around 47 million students at the end of the last century. However, new schools that are not traditional public schools have seen explosive growth. Private school enrollment had grown to over 5 million by the 1999–2000 academic year. By the fall of 2002, 2,700 charter schools had opened, an increase of 900 schools in just two years. Charter schools served over 575,000 in 2002–2003. In 1999, 850,000 students were being home schooled, equivalent to the number of students in public education in the state of Minnesota. This represents 1.7 percent of all students, and 82 percent of these children are exclusively home schooled. The percentage growth in this population has been double-digit for the past several years and is expected to continue to grow over the next several years. In 2001–2002, it was estimated that 50,000 students were enrolled in virtual schools, equivalent to the entire public school system of Minneapolis. This represents a 33 percent increase in a single year. Many educators or, as they are called in this book, *educational entrepreneurs* will be involved in the opening of thousands of new schools over the next decade.

The fundamental premise of this book is that educational leaders who are trying to engage in the current transformation of America's education system can learn important lessons from traditional entrepreneurs. But what do entrepreneurs have to teach leaders trying to start up new schools? Why try to learn from entrepreneurs? Isn't the most important concern that of the curriculum and quality of the staffing in a school? If a school gets that right, isn't it bound to succeed? After all, schools are not businesses.

In fact, new schools behave just like any new organization, and more and more are being formed as for-profit businesses. Change is the source of the opportunities that have created the swell of new schools, and change is the source of almost any new spurt of entrepreneurial energy in any particular business sector. New schools follow the same patterns and have the same basic risks that can lead to failure just as any new business. They also fail for the same types of reasons. For example, 92 percent of failures in charter schools have been linked to nonacademic rationale. The primary reasons for failure, in order of occurrence, were finances, mismanagement, and inappropriate facilities. All are common problems in any failure during the early stages of an entrepreneurial organization's development. Only 8 percent of charter school failures were a result of not getting their academics in order.

The entrepreneurial process has been applied to any number of organizational types. Early on, the primary focus was on traditional business start-ups. In the 1980s, a handful of pioneering universities began to offer a few courses in entrepreneurship. Today, the vast majority of universities that offer business curriculum now teach entrepreneurship. Some even offer majors in entrepreneurship. Recently, the lessons learned from more traditional entrepreneurs have been applied to more nontraditional settings. For example, a movement in the 1990s saw the application of entrepreneurial management techniques to nonprofits, primarily those with a social service orientation. This movement is now known as *social entrepreneurship*, and it has spawned dozens of conferences and books addressing the entrepreneurial nature of new social service nonprofits. The author, his colleagues, and others across the country have recognized that school start-ups also can benefit from the same transfer of knowledge from the field of entrepreneurship to school administration and management.

ENTREPRENEURSHIP 101

Originally, the study of entrepreneurship began as a study of the characteristics of the people who became entrepreneurs. The goal of these studies was to determine the personal traits that made for successful entrepreneurs. After all, everyone knew that entrepreneurs were just born to be entrepreneurs. Only someone with a high tolerance or even a high attraction to risk taking would willingly start a business knowing that 80 to 90 percent of start-ups fail. However, a few scholars began to study not who entrepreneurs were but rather what they did. From this, remarkable changes began to emerge in what was written about entrepreneurs. Those entrepreneurs who followed certain processes and made decisions using certain protocols proved to have much higher success rates. With that in mind, those of us in business schools with an interest in entrepreneurship began to teach these findings to those who aspired to become entrepreneurs. We found, time after time, that those who were properly trained to handle the challenges of entrepreneurial ventures no longer failed but actually *succeeded* at a rate of 80 to 90 percent.

Entrepreneurs are most often trained using a model that examines the life cycle of the business. There are certain issues that are unique to each stage of a business as it develops, and skills and techniques apply to each of these stages. Figure 1.1 displays the life cycle model of a new venture.

The prelaunch phase is concerned with critical issues that face any start-up before the doors are actually opened for the first day of operation.

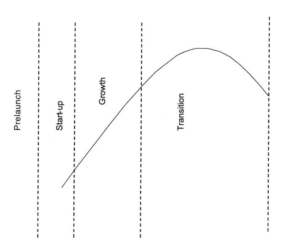

Figure 1.1.   Life Cycle of an Entrepreneurial Venture

It is generally recommended that entrepreneurs proceed in two distinct steps during the preventure phase. The first step examines the basic feasibility of the new venture. The goal is the following: If this new venture (in this case, school) is going to fail, it is much better that it fails on paper before many resources have been committed, any people are actually hired, and relationships with potential families are established. Most entrepreneurs are tempted to skip this step. They are so passionate about their ideas and so committed to them that they are absolutely convinced that they cannot fail. However, failure is the likely outcome if they do not objectively answer three basic questions:

1. *Is this school really something the entrepreneur is ready to commit him- or herself to at this time?* This is a more complex question than it may at first appear. When working with entrepreneurs in any type of setting, I use the metaphor of falling in love. After all, it is easy to fall in love: Almost everyone has done it before. The challenge is to determine whether the person with whom one is in love is the person with whom to spend the rest of one's life. This requires careful and deliberate consideration, for impulsiveness in love is wrought with danger. The same is true with entrepreneurship. We can easily be consumed with passion for an idea, but more level heads should prevail before actually committing to starting up any new venture. Will this school be able to meet the founder's income needs? Will it allow the continued pursuit of interests outside of work, such as family, hobbies, church, community groups, and so forth? Is this a school that I can continue to be passionate about over the longer term? Will it continue to be *fun*? Does this school match my skills and experiences? Chapter 2 addresses this issue as it lays out the importance of a clearly defined vision for a new school.
2. *Is there really a market for this new school?* Are there enough families that will want to send their children to this school to make it a viable entity over time? This question addresses the fallacy in thinking that is best described by the phrase "If we build it, they will come." Because we are so passionate about our ideas, we assume that *everyone* will obviously share our passion. However, what is so obviously wonderful to the founder may not be

the same for everyone else. The entrepreneur should take the time to test the basic validity of the idea. Do potential clients see this as the same great idea as the entrepreneur? And if it is a great idea, is it great enough to motivate them to send their children to the school? This is particularly true for innovative, new school ideas. For example, a school founder in the southeastern United States created a therapeutic preschool that he hoped would have just as many mentally healthy children as it did those with mental illnesses. His vision was to establish a school where both groups of children could learn from each other. He soon found that even the most enlightened parents were not willing to place their mentally healthy children in such a school.

3. *Can we operate this school with adequate margins to meet the needs of everyone involved in the school?* That is, is the basic model of this school one that results in "bills being paid"? As many managers in nonprofits preach to their staff, "If there is no margin, we have no mission." Every organization needs to think beyond the notion of simply breaking even. Positive cash flows (that is, more money coming in during the year than going out), whether they create profits or simply create surpluses, should be the goal of any organization. Positive cash flows do not simply happen. Some businesses can never create adequate margins. If analyzed properly, this should be evident *before* the decision to launch a new venture is even made. Chapter 3 examines the issues of market and margin using a basic feasibility approach to examining a potential new venture.

If the initial answers to these questions are negative, it does not mean that the entrepreneur should abandon the idea. This first step of the pre-venture phase is often iterative. The entrepreneur may need to test and reformulate the idea several times before moving ahead to the next step. But if the initial evaluation remains negative, even after repeated attempts to refine the concept, the idea should not be taken any further. It may not be a permanent tabling of the idea, however. For example, the problem may be that the funding is not adequate right now but that it could improve in the future. Or families may not be ready to gravitate to such a new concept in sufficient numbers until they see more evidence of its success.

Once the basic soundness of the idea has been demonstrated, the entrepreneur should move on to the second step of preventure phase: planning. Many entrepreneurs rush prematurely into planning. It is essential that the first step described previously be fully evaluated before planning begins. A business plan is the document that challenges the entrepreneur to completely think through all the details of the concept. Just as with the previous step, the business plan development should be viewed as a "go or no go" step in preventure development. If the plan does not result in a supportive conclusion for the new school, the idea should be stopped. Chapters 4 to 9 provide the details of the business plan process.

If the idea for the school makes it past the preventure phase with adequate support for its creation, then the challenges of the actual start-up begin. How well will the team implement the plan as it was developed? What changes will be needed in the plan based on new information or due to changing conditions? The start-up phase is an extremely stressful time for all involved, so the better prepared everyone is, the better the chances are that the school will begin with a positive launch. This book examines the start-up process and presents some of the issues that need careful attention during the early beginnings of an organization.

More businesses fail during growth than during the start-up. Yet growth is a time when too many leaders fail to continue the diligent planning that helped make the start-up successful. Furthermore, unlike some organizations, schools often face significant growth from the very beginning. Successfully building a culture is critical to managing growth (this is discussed in chapter 10). Successfully managing the growth process requires effective leadership, developing systems, and preparing for the transitions of the founders. All these topics are examined in chapter 11.

APPLYING BUSINESS TERMINOLOGY TO SCHOOLS

Some business terms may seem like a foreign language to those who have spent their careers in educational settings. However, once we get past the connotations that some of these terms carry and understand the concepts they are describing, it will be demonstrated that most have utility in educational start-ups just as they do in traditional business start-ups. It also is important to keep in mind that schools are beginning to take all types of organizational forms. Any number of nonprofit and for-profit schools with a wide variety of differing orientations can be found. Public school systems are seeing competitive entrepreneurial school start-ups from within their own systems with the explosion of charter schools and the emergence of new organizations such as independent professional teacher cooperatives. This book is designed to help all forms of start-up schools, for their challenges are all basically alike.

A new school may be the outcome of the efforts of a single person, a small group, or even a larger collection of people, including groups of parents or teachers. All will be considered founders no matter how many are involved in the start-up of a particular school. For the sake of simplicity, this book may at times refer to a single founder in its discussion. The founder is also referred to as the leader and the entrepreneur. The intent is not to confuse the reader but to highlight the multiple roles these people play: founder, entrepreneur, *and* leader.

This book assumes that all schools, no matter what legal organizational form, should have the same ultimate financial goal: positive cash flow. Too many entrepreneurs, in all settings, find that breaking even (that is, having just enough cash coming in to pay for what needs to go out) is a major milestone. But simply breaking even, for any type of organization, is inherently risky. Educational entrepreneurs often do not think that breaking even or meeting a balanced budget will require a significant change in thinking. Why?

The reason is really quite simple. Many educational entrepreneurs come out of public school administration. What is the financial goal in such a setting? To break even, of course. A school is budgeted a certain amount of funding—the cash in for their organization. The job of the administrator is primarily to not go over the predetermined budget, as doing so will lead the superintendent and the school board to have concerns about that administrator's management skills. On the other hand, most administrators are careful not to leave any allocated funding unspent. That money will go away and may even result in lower allocations for the next year, depending on the budget process used in the school. There is really no such thing as a surplus in this situation.

In a freestanding school, however, breaking even is very risky. An unforeseen event of any magnitude (and life always seems to create unforeseen events) can put the school in financial distress or result in hardship for the school. For example, one start-up school had a very tight budget and should have broken even if all went according to plan. Unfortunately, events began to unfold that put the school potentially into serious jeopardy. More students than expected decided not to attend just as the school year began. Since this school got its revenues from the students it enrolled, that loss created an immediate strain. Then a teacher who was no longer needed had to be terminated. She filed a legal grievance that required that the school pay legal fees. In addition, transportation costs turned out to be higher than planned. Fortunately, the school found the means to survive, but not without some painful pay cuts and even a few layoffs.

Clearly, a for-profit school has the need to take in more than it spends—that is the nature of profit. But there are many other reasons to strive for positive cash flow, whether a school is for-profit, non-profit, or even an independent public school, such as a charter school. (Although they get much of their funding through the public schools, charter schools in most states are financially independent entities and can, and in many cases are expected to, operate with a surplus each year.) The three most important reasons to strive for positive cash flow rather than just a break-even budget, are as follows:

1. *Future capital needs:* Positive cash flow can be accumulated and used to support part or even all of future capital needs, such as major new equipment purchases or building expansion or renovations.
2. *Creating breathing room for the unexpected:* Operating with a positive cash flow, a school can absorb variations from the plan with little noticeable effect.
3. *Managing the "lumpiness" of cash flow:* Cash tends to go out in relatively equal amounts each month. Payroll tends to be fairly constant, rent is usually fixed, and so on. However, cash coming in is anything but predictable. Private schools find that some parents get behind on tuition payments, and state appropriations can get delayed in settings such as charter schools. A good practice is to have the equivalent of at least one month's operating expenses

in a reserve account for this purpose. Some nonprofits have up to a year's worth, so that if funding gets interrupted or severely curtailed, they have time to adjust how they will operate going forward. Clearly, such reserves take time and may not be possible in the first year of operation in most schools.

Therefore, it is assumed that positive cash flow is the goal. Positive cash flow will have a variety of purposes, only one of which is profit in a for-profit school. It has to be noted that many nonprofits in reality create excess cash flow that benefits the founder and/or leadership. Excess cash flow can lead to increased salaries and perks, such as extensive travel to meetings and conventions. Positive cash flow does not—and should never—come at the expense of quality education. But, as with health care, it can and should be the outcome of a well-managed, high-quality school. Part of being well managed is being financially responsible and fiscally prudent.

Calling a student, a family, or a public sector entity a *customer* is not intended to be demeaning in any way. It should not be seen as cheapening the important function of educating our youth. In fact, using the metaphor of the customer to understand what it takes to get students into the school in the first place is not only useful but also may be fundamentally necessary in the changing marketplace that is education in America. Therefore, this book uses the term *customer* but does so only with the most positive connotations intended.

In short, since start-up schools are realizing the need to act more businesslike, this book uses common business terms to make its points. From experience with many start-up schools, I have found that once the initial discomfort of hearing such terms used in this context passes, educational entrepreneurs embrace this language, and the skills and techniques that serve as its foundation, as being critical to their successes. They even take great joy in thinking of themselves as entrepreneurs, particularly successful entrepreneurs.

HOW TO USE THIS BOOK

This book is written to be both a primer (that is, something to be read before undertaking the start-up of a new school) and a reference for any independent school. The lessons of the start-up seem to recur over time and, for many entrepreneurs, never completely go away. In addition, once they catch the entrepreneurial bug, many educational entrepreneurs find fulfillment in working with multiple start-up schools over time. This book is also intended to be a refresher for these "serial" educational entrepreneurs.

CHAPTER 2

Defining the Vision

In general, most founders of new schools have a very clear understanding of the schools they want to create. For example, when Dr. Karen Rusthoven founded Community of Peace Academy in 1995, a charter school located in Minnesota, she envisioned a school that would replicate "all of the exceptionally good qualities that Catholic schools have, without violating the law of separation of church and state." Dr. Rusthoven did not wish to impose her faith in a public school setting. In fact, she is Lutheran and is married to a pastor. She had an extremely positive experience early in her career as a teacher in a Catholic school and became passionate about what she had encountered in that school. She captured this experience and used it to create her vision for an alternative to public schools. This was her *vision.* She had a clear picture of what the school would be like before the first student was enrolled and the first teacher was hired.

Thus, a leader's view of what a business concept (or, in this case, a school) can become is called the *vision.* Although most school founders have an idea of their vision in their own mind, the vision is often incomplete. In addition, the vision often is not defined well enough to be able to clearly articulate it to others. As the school develops, the leader will need to communicate this vision to state regulators, sources of funding, parents, teachers, staff, and students. This chapter defines the key components of a completely developed vision statement, characteristics of an effective vision, and how new school leaders should effectively use their vision to establish and grow their schools.

COMPONENTS OF VISION

The goal in developing a vision is to develop it to the point that it can be written down and easily communicated to others. This can be a much bigger challenge than it first appears. Many times when asked to communicate a vision for a new venture, be it a new school or a new entrepreneurial business, the founder is unable to communicate the vision easily. Although it may be clear in their minds, translating that into a written or even a verbal format can be quite daunting. Many founding entrepreneurs lack a clear focus and may have only a vague notion of what they intend to create. For example, "I want to create a safe place for kids that offers a top-quality education." As will be seen, this vision statement lacks many of the key components and characteristics that would make it effective. On the other hand, the founder's vision may be much too broad to be realistic. For example, "From our very beginning, we will offer a complete educational system, from early childhood education through high school, which integrates e-learning, in-home options, language immersion, cutting-edge technology education, and a full array of extracurricular options, including athletics." Such a vision, although noble in its intent, becomes seemingly unrealistic to accomplish. It promises too much for too many too soon to be realistic. A well-developed vision should become a meaningful statement of purpose within a proven format.

Entrepreneurs have found that the most effective vision statements have four main components: core values, a statement of purpose and focus, a well-defined mission statement, and general goals tied to the founder's aspirations for the school.

Core Values

The founder's core values should be at the heart of the vision statement. These core values provide the foundation for the culture of the organization as it grows. Such values are defined by the ethical principles and morals that the founder intends to bring to the business.

For some schools, the group, organization, or community that supports the start-up defines core values. For example, a religious-based private school draws its core values from its religious tradition. A Baptist school will have very clear values that are derived from the core elements of that faith, just as would a Jewish school, a Catholic school, and so forth. A charter school started by a particular community group, such as an immigrant population, will draw its core values from that population's culture. In other instances, founders may have their own core values that they wish to use to attract a specific group of people, possibly from a particular political point of view, such as the free schools of the 1970s that rejected traditional authority structures and hierarchy.

Some founders may not draw from such a clear cultural foundation or heritage. In such cases, core values are still important. The founder's values will shape how the organization will treat its employees, its students and parents, its suppliers, and the broader community in which it operates. For example, a private, for-profit organization located in the southern United States ran a residential boarding school for children with mental illnesses. The founders consciously brought their core values to all their facilities, including this school. They believed that all their resident students should be treated with dignity and should be challenged to achieve the most that their abilities allowed. This value shaped who they hired (all employees were expected to share these values), their curriculum, and their policies and procedures. These values could be observed in the day-to-day interactions between staff and residents. Another value was a strong commitment and sense of obligation to employees. The organization had a "no layoff" policy despite the fluctuations that naturally occurred in numbers of residents. One final value was that they believed in open and honest communication. This was evident not only in the organization but also in how the staff interacted with neighbors to their facility. When a child eloped from the grounds, the staff immediately notified all neighbors. (Eloping, in this use of the term, refers to running away. It is a common euphemism in residential schools, particularly for those that treat children with mental illnesses.) Although at first this created uneasiness, over time it proved to create an atmosphere of trust that defined a very positive relationship with most of their neighbors. All these core values were well-known by all in the organization because the founders deliberately and consciously articulated them. Such values will become the cornerstone of the school's culture. An example of the importance of deliberately communicating a vision can be seen in a private school's start-up experience:

> One of our biggest challenges, perhaps, was the fact that most of our kids, parents, and teachers were brought in from 25 different former schools and it was hard to try and establish a sense of community. Getting everyone to have the same common vision at St. Ambrose was a trick. The key to our success was to let the students, parents, and staff know the values and rules of St. Ambrose, and after a couple of months of constantly reminding people of these, a sense of community was established at our school. (Mathew Metz, principal, St. Ambrose Catholic School, Woodbury, Minnesota)

The role and the importance of a well-communicated vision are discussed further later in this chapter and are reexamined in chapter 10 as it relates to managing the school as it grows.

Purpose and Focus

Recently, a consultant came to the author seeking help in improving his own consulting business. Although a well-known and well-connected former politician, he was having trouble building his consulting practice. He had been certain that with his knowledge and with the people he knew, his business would be booming as soon as he opened up his practice. When asked to define the nature of his consulting practice, he began to talk—and talk and talk. Twenty minutes later, I asked him to stop and let me ask a question. I asked that if he had only thirty seconds to explain the focus of his consulting practice, what would he say? He was stumped, finally realizing that he had to work on this if anyone was to know what he did in his business. He had to define the statement, "If we need _____, we should call _____."

Such a clear statement of purpose is sometimes called an "elevator answer." If you meet a potential customer or a potential investor in an elevator and had only the ride up ten stories to tell him what your business is all about, how would you describe it? A clear statement of purpose should define the fundamental reason of being in this business or, in the case of this book, for opening this new school. For example, a Minnesota charter school has developed a clear understanding of their purpose. They describe their purpose as being "dedicated to a community based, holistic approach to education through quality academics by utilizing Latino culture in an environment of 'familia' and community." They have found that this statement speaks clearly and directly to their teachers, staff, parents, students, and the broader community. Each major component of this statement has meaning. "Community based," for example, indicates that the school is to be fully integrated and will clearly serve the community within which it operates. This is carried out by their involvement in community activities, their openness to regularly encouraging community activities to take place within the school building, and their encouragement that community members be actively engaged in the school's operations. It also is clear from this statement that all activities within the school—curricular, cocurricular, and extracurricular—will be integrated within the context of the Latino culture.

A statement of purpose should meet four important characteristics. First, it should be *clear*. There is very little room for ambiguity in a statement of purpose. The example from the charter school in the previous paragraph makes a clear statement as to what the fundamental nature of the school and its basic purpose are all about.

Second, the statement of purpose should be *consistent* with what actually happens in the school. In the previous example, the vision for the school would lose all its impact if the statement of purpose were not consistent with what was actually occurring within the school. Consistency builds credibility.

Third, the statement of purpose should be *compelling*. It should be strong enough to motivate everyone associated with the school to believe in, and act consistently with, its intentions. It should be compelling enough that members of the organization personalize it as their own and so that, even when times are difficult in the school, it reminds everyone of their shared purpose. For example, start-up schools often face periods of enrollment that fall short of expectations, creating a cash flow crisis. This may require everyone in the school to manage their scarce budget more carefully than planned. A compelling statement of purpose can not only make such times bearable but can also galvanize the commitment of all to make sure the school endures and fulfills the vision.

Finally, the statement of purpose should have *continuity.* Although staff may change and students come and go, a statement of purpose should endure over time. As will be seen in later chapters, a school may need to change its place in the market or even its approaches to education, but its basic purpose should endure beyond almost any of these changes. The longer the purpose endures, the stronger its impact and the greater its legitimacy. However, change will eventually come to all things if enough time passes. For example, a school that was established for a particular immigrant community or religious faith may over time need to reconsider its purpose if demographics change too drastically. For example, an after-school educational center was established to serve the inner-city African American population in a neighborhood located in a large metropolitan city. Over just ten years, the population in this neighborhood changed from predominantly African American to almost exclusively Asian immigrants. Clearly in this case, the purpose of this center had to change to meet the needs of its new constituency if it was to stay relevant for its neighborhood. However, a statement of purpose normally changes only under extraordinary circumstances and after very careful and deliberate consideration of the impact of such a change.

Mission

Once core values and a statement of purpose are defined, the entrepreneur develops the final component of vision, which is a *mission statement.* A mission statement takes the generalized understanding of purpose and creates a more explicit direction for the school. A mission statement defines specifically what we are doing (our product or service) and for whom we are doing it (our market) and sometimes includes how we intend to do it (our processes). An example for a hypothetical Internet-based school might read as follows:

> We offer a comprehensive curriculum grounded in sound fundamental education for students in grades K through 12 who are home schooled using the latest asynchronous Internet-based educational software platforms.

This mission defines product, market, and processes in a single, concise statement.

For most schools, the market needs to be more narrowly defined, and the process may not be relevant to include (that is, a standard classroom school is so common that it need not be indicated in a mission statement for such a school) or may focus more on curricular or pedagogical models. The Latino charter school described earlier in this chapter has the following mission statement:

> Academia Cesar Chavez is dedicated to providing a quality education for Hispanic youth and their families in St. Paul (Minnesota) that prepares critically thinking, socially competent, values driven, and culturally aware learners by utilizing Latino cultural values in an environment of "familia" and community.

The "product" is a quality education, the "market" is the Hispanic community in St. Paul, and the "process" is utilizing Latino cultural values.

In many organizations, the mission statement is the only part of the vision to be documented and used in writing. However, a complete understanding of the vision requires explicit treatment of values and purpose in addition to the more tangible aspects of the mission statement.

Goals and Aspirations

The final component of vision includes the goals and aspirations for the organization and its founders. The goals and aspirations for the organization should be more generalized, as they often address more subjective and long-term considerations, such as reputation and quality. For example, a new parochial school may have as its goal to be the leading faith-based school in the metropolitan area within five years. Goals also can pertain to such indicators as size, scope of offerings, comprehensiveness of ages served, demographics of the student body, college placement data, test scores, and so forth. Goals for the organization included within a vision statement should be of a longer time frame. Certainly there will be goals and objectives that are more focused on the shorter term that are critically important, but goals within the vision statement should be those that may take several years to accomplish.

Goals are examined in further detail in chapter 4, where the format and process for developing the action plan are discussed.

The personal goals and aspirations of the founder can be equally important. If the founders do not actively address their own goals and aspirations as they relate to the new school, they may not have the ability to sustain the energy, drive, and passion needed to lead the new school to the point where it is successful and can be a sustainable entity. For example, the founder may intend to lead the school only until it is up to full occupancy or when the funding is healthy and sustainable from year to year. This goal will need to be integrated into the growth and development of the school. If not, the founder may stay on too long, well beyond his or her skills and motivation. Many entrepreneurs fail to recognize their own limitations in managing their growing businesses and stay in charge too long. This can be equally true with an entrepreneur in education. Although the founding educational entrepreneur may feel a strong sense of commitment and responsibility, it is not unreasonable to integrate his or her own aspirations and goals into the planning of the school. The school will need the founder's full energy and commitment.

Cornwall and Carter (2000) developed a self-assessment for entrepreneurs to help ensure that their own aspirations and values are integrated into their new ventures. The questions in the self-assessment are equally important for an educational entrepreneur to consider as he or she develops the vision for a new school. The following is a summary of some of the key questions related to the founder's aspirations from this self-assessment:

What gets you excited, gives you energy, and motivates you to excel?

What do you like to do with your time?

What drains energy from you in the work you do?

What drains energy from you in personal relationships?

How do you measure success in your personal life in terms of family, friends and relationships, personal interests, hobbies, and your contributions to the community and to society?

What do you consider success in your career, both short- and long-term?

What are your specific goals for your personal life regarding family, friends and relationships, personal interests, hobbies, and your contributions to the community and to society?

What are your goals for your career in terms of income, lifestyle, wealth, free time, recognition, and your impact on the community?

What do you want to be doing in one year? In five years? In ten years? At retirement?

Entrepreneurs in any setting can benefit from honest and periodic evaluation of these issues, even after the organization is up and running. Situations change, and it is important to reflect on these changes and what they may mean for the person and the school. It is best to take the time to sit down and write a reflective response to these questions before the school is created and about once each year thereafter.

VISION AS A FOUNDATION FOR CULTURE

The vision is the foundation of the organizational culture. The founder begins to shape the culture from his or her very first actions and decisions. The culture begins as a reflection of the values of the founder. Therefore, it is crucial to fully understand the concept of organizational culture at the very beginning of any new entity. Organizational culture can be defined as the basics beliefs and assumptions about what the school is all about, how its members should behave, and how it defines its purpose. A critical function of culture is to communicate what is considered right and wrong, and again this starts at the very beginning of the school. Some ethical standards are written down in ethical codes, while others are unwritten norms that are learned over time. All the ethical standards, both those written and those understood though tradition, help define the core values of the organizational culture. Building and managing an effective culture is one of the key elements for successfully managing the growth of a school over time. Chapter 10 is devoted to the discussion of this important topic.

SUMMARY

This chapter has examined the process of creating a vision for a new school. This is the first step in ensuring that an idea for a new school is truly a viable opportunity that can be sustained over time. The second step is to develop an initial feasibility assessment of the school. This step, which examines the potential market for the school and its ability to generate an adequate operating margin, is discussed in the next chapter.

CHAPTER 3

The Initial Feasibility Assessment

The fundamental goal of a feasibility assessment is to identify any and all possible flaws with an idea for a new school. While many creative ideas might be considered, only a certain number of these are true opportunities with a reasonable probability of success. Experienced entrepreneurs refer to this process as *failing on paper.* If an idea has inherent flaws, it is much better to fail on paper during the feasibility analysis or during the second stage of evaluation, the planning phase (discussed in part 2 of this book), than to commit the resources, reputations, and trust of funders and families to a doomed idea.

Any entrepreneur is naturally excited about his or her new idea and would not be willing to commit the time it takes to even get to this point if there were not a growing passion for the idea. But the passion one has for a new idea compared to the wisdom of whether to pursue it is not that different from romance. Just because two people fall in love does not necessarily mean they should commit to marriage. It takes much more than love for a successful long-term relationship to thrive. Yet that is exactly what an entrepreneur is doing when rushing headlong into a new venture without thoughtful and careful evaluation of the wisdom of doing so.

Feasibility analysis is not a thorough development of the idea into a formal plan. Rather, it is a systematic analysis of the two most fundamental questions necessary to objectively evaluate any idea: Is there an adequate market for the idea? and Can it be operated with an acceptable margin of positive cash flow? If the answer to either of these questions does not support moving ahead, it does not necessarily mean that the idea should be abandoned. This phase in the development of a new school should be approached as an iterative process. The idea may undergo several refinements until it starts to make sense to develop a full plan. However, even if after several refinements the answer to the questions of market and margin are still negative, then the idea, no matter how well-intentioned and no matter how much passion lies behind it, should be abandoned.

EVALUATING THE MARKET

Never start a school just because *you* are excited about a new idea. An entrepreneur must have *customers* or, in this case, the *families and their children* who also are excited. Failure to evaluate the market is one of the single biggest mistakes any entrepreneur can make. The initial market evaluation addresses three basic questions:

1. *Who is the customer?* Although this question may seem trivial, it has actually proven to be a major stumbling block for many would-be entrepreneurs. The intended market may be fairly narrow, such as a charter school for children of Hmong families. Or the intended market may be fairly broad, such as a private school with a special emphasis on science and math. Whatever the case, the intended market should be as clearly and specifically defined as possible. All definitions of the market, including geographic, demographic, grade level, and special interests, should be understood before progressing any further with an investigation of the market. This is one area that may need to be adjusted if the basic feasibility is not supported. The market may need to be broadened, narrowed, or in some other way redefined.

2. *Does the customer need our service?* The ideal market is one that already perceives a need for the new type of school under consideration. Even a well-defined demographic group may not perceive that it needs its own school apart from the public schools already available. Often entrepreneurs are much more aware of specific needs than is the general population, creating a huge hurdle for the entrepreneur to overcome. They must build awareness

and a sense of perceived need, and this can take time and money. These are two commodities that are usually in short supply in any start-up. Therefore, it is important early in the evaluation of an idea for a new school to determine whether the market is receptive without too much effort to inform and even educate about the need.

3. *Are there enough potential customers to make the idea workable?* Even though there may already be an awareness of the need for a new school, it is critical to determine whether there is enough demand to make it a viable entity. For example, assume that a group wants to start an elementary school for a specific immigrant group in a community. They want to have at least one class of about twenty students for each grade level since they believe that this would be the minimum enrollment to support their efforts. They are passionate about the idea, and there appears to be interest within this community. However, some basic demographic research shows that this immigrant group is small. In fact, they would have to attract the children from over two-thirds of the immigrant group's families to come close to filling one class per grade level. Although it may not be impossible, it likely would be difficult to reach this percentage from any group no matter how enthusiastic they seem. A certain percentage will not want to leave their current schools for any number of reasons. On the other hand, if the school identified a large market and only a small percentage of that market would need to be interested in attending the new school, its chances of reaching the necessary enrollment levels are much better. This is the concept known in business as *market share*, which is discussed further in chapters 5 and 6.

Although a thorough and systematic examination of the market is not part of feasibility analysis, it is important to make any evaluation with real data. One type of data that can be extremely enlightening is that from entrepreneurs in other geographic areas. In these cases, entrepreneurs come across an idea that worked in another setting that they believe can be applied to their own setting. For example, one of the first wilderness camp boarding schools was the Salesmanship Club Youth

Camp outside Dallas, Texas. This residential program for troubled youth, founded in 1946, inspired many other entrepreneurs across the country to develop similar residential programs. Many of these entrepreneurs were welcomed to Texas to visit the camp and were offered great insight into what worked and what did not. Much of this information related to what type of children the program attracted, how they found out about the program, and how the children were referred. Such market information proved invaluable to other program founders as they examined the potential for their own markets. Directly observing what works and why it works in other markets can be relatively easy data to collect. As in this example, many entrepreneurs are eager to share their experiences with others as long as the visitors will not be direct competitors.

Another good source of initial data can be discovered from similar populations within the same or a nearby market. Many charter schools look to existing charter schools that cater to a different population subgroup as models for the group they want to attract. For example, a charter school for Hmong families has proven successful, so it may be a good model for Somalian families in the same city. Both populations were found to be of similar size, and both seem to have a strong desire to maintain elements of their culture. Therefore, a charter school's being successful within one of these groups is a fairly good initial predictor of success for the other. More extensive evaluation should follow, but this would be at least a reasonable initial assessment of feasibility.

Sometimes an idea has strong demand that is fairly obvious without much evaluation. Such was the case for the new Catholic school being considered in Woodbury, Minnesota:

> Our parish was established in March of 1998. When the parish was formed, they decided that having a Catholic school in the area was a priority. At the time, Woodbury was the fastest growing city in Minnesota. The nearest Catholic school was [several miles away] in Stillwater or Hastings, but nothing in Woodbury. This meant that demographically we didn't do a lot of research because we could clearly see that a Catholic school was needed in this area of Minnesota. (Mathew Metz, principal, St. Ambrose Catholic School)

The decision to pay for a school is sometimes separated from the actual families whose children will be attending the school. For example, charter school funding comes from public school dollars. Therefore, any assessment of feasibility should include not only the prospective families but also the decision makers within the public school and possibly state education systems that make the ultimate funding decisions on charter schools. Many of these decision makers are accessible and very willing to talk about new ideas. They have a wealth of experience with other new schools and can help one understand the political landscape that must be navigated while opening a new school. The entrepreneur should not focus on persuasion in initial conversations with decision makers but should listen very carefully to gather information about concerns and issues that will need to be addressed should the idea move ahead into a more formalized proposal.

Another source of preliminary data to support the market feasibility can come from secondary research. Population trends, policy decisions, and legislative initiatives can all provide information supporting a new school. New sources of funding, new housing projects, and new real estate developments are all examples of information that may indicate a receptive environment for new and innovative school ideas.

Experience in the market may provide enough supporting data to suggest market feasibility. One charter school founder had worked with children in her target population for several years before deciding to open her new elementary school:

Through the University of St. Thomas we had run an after-school summer program for ten years focusing on the education of Latino children. Families that we had been serving from that program began asking us to start a school based on the same concept. After several requests we began looking at the growing Latino population in the state of Minnesota. The median age of the Latino population is twenty-three, which is quite young. This means we have young people that are going to be getting married and having children. Looking both at the statistics and having requests from members of the community, we realized a school of this type was needed. (Ramona Rosales, executive director, Academia Cesar Chavez, St. Paul, Minnesota)

Some ideas can be best described as truly innovative. For these ideas, there are no examples from other markets, no models that directly support market feasibility of such ideas. Assessing the market for such ideas may, at first, seem impossible. However, a method used by many entrepreneurs is to examine parallel start-ups that are based on the same fundamental trend in the market or even a similar trend with similar impact on the market. For example, the first companies to support home schooling via the Internet were truly pioneers in education. Since no one had tried such a business, there was very little direct evidence that it would be feasible. However, while education provided using only the Internet was slowly gaining ground in all levels of education, using the Internet as a complement to traditional classroom teaching was catching on. Thus, moving such a model into home schooling at least had a parallel, and research showed that these families were already beginning to use the Internet as an educational tool. The product would need to be structured completely differently in almost every aspect from traditional supplemental classroom Internet services that allowed mainly for displaying lecture notes, on-line discussions, and on-line testing. For home schooling, the product would need to link to entire textbooks and curricula in addition to support materials and tools for parents of home-schooled children. Thus, there were parallels and evidence of a receptive market for this type of new venture.

NO MARGIN, NO MISSION

Whether a school is established as a nonprofit or a for-profit, its founders must be concerned with the cash flow of the organization. The second question of the feasibility assessment refers to the ability of a proposed school to generate enough revenues to more than offset expenses necessary to run the school while providing for future needs. Just as was the case with the market assessment, the financial aspect of a feasibility assessment does not involve a fully developed set of budgets or financial projections. Rather, a general sense of the economic viability of the proposed school is the goal at this point. As with the initial market assessment, existing schools can serve as excellent models for financial viability. Associations also have useful general data on both costs and potential revenues. The entrepreneur should make an initial financial assessment using this type of data as a baseline. Variations based on pedagogical model, staffing assumptions, local costs, and programming will need to be considered to adjust the figures of these other schools' experiences.

Revenues for schools can come from a myriad of sources. Many schools develop a portfolio of revenue sources to support their operation (the specifics of revenue forecasting are discussed in chapter 9). At this point, the entrepreneur needs to get a sense of the general types of funding that may be available to support the operations of the school. This can include tuition, public education allocations, grants, endowments, and so forth. Some schools may have access to unique funding sources. For example, charter schools are eligible for access to grants from a variety of sources. Private parochial schools may receive funds from affiliated religious organizations. Certain foundations support schools with specific themes that match the general mission of the foundation's benefactors. At this stage, the objective is to develop an understanding of what funding sources are possible and what general level of support can be expected from these sources.

It also is important to understand the basic cost structure for the envisioned school, which begins identifying the typical general costs associated with any school. The usual staffing and space requirements, as well as typical operating costs such as food, supplies, and transportation, are included. Then the entrepreneur should begin to assess expenses that may be unique to the new school. That is, many innovative schools have features that add additional costs both to the start-up and to operations. Several basic questions should be addressed. Are there specific or even unique expenses that need to be considered for the school? This might include special staffing requirements, such as low student-to-teacher ratios. Are there space requirements that will add to the cost of the school? Examples of this include labs for science and math schools, practice rooms for music schools, or dormitories and other special facilities for residential schools. Are there ancillary expenses that may need to be considered? Such expenses could include special education staff, mental health staff, nursing staff, or technical specialists, such as in information technology. On the basis of the assessment of the additional expenses required, the entrepreneur can evaluate the *relative* costs associated with the planned school. Is it fairly standard? If so, its expenses should be fairly predictable by using existing schools as a model. If it has unique features, the costs of these must be planned for when assessing the financial feasibility.

Once the entrepreneur has a general understanding of the potential sources of revenues and the relative expenses of the proposed school, a general assessment of the financial feasibility can be ascertained. Such an assessment cannot be made independently of the previous market feasibility assessment. That is, financial feasibility depends on demand because of the way that expenses behave.

Generally, there are two types of expenses: fixed and variable. *Fixed expenses* remain constant no matter what the enrollment in the school. Such expenses include rent and administrative salaries. *Variable expenses* include those costs that vary with the number of students enrolled in the school. Variable expenses include costs such as meals and classroom supplies. The single biggest expense in most schools is teacher and classroom support staff salaries. While these expenses do not vary dollar for dollar with enrollment, they generally still behave like a variable expense since they go up as enrollments go up and can be treated as such for the purposes of the feasibility analysis.

Each increase in enrollment leads to an increase in revenues (tuition, state aid, and so forth) and an increase in variable expenses. The difference between these two figures is the *operating margin* that each new student creates. For example, if each new student generates $1,000 in revenue and costs the school $800 in variable expenses, then the operating margin per student is $200. Breakeven occurs when enough students are enrolled that the total of the operating margins they generate totals the fixed expenses. If the fixed expenses in the school in this example are $20,000, the school will need 100 students to break even. In this case, there will be 100 students, each accounting for $200 in operating margin for a total of $20,000. If the market analysis indicates that it would be very difficult to reach 100 students, then the feasibility of this school is called into question. It is critical for the educational entrepreneur to understand the behavior of expenses in their proposed school. Each start-up can have its own specific circumstances that need to be clearly understood and planned for.

Assume that the previous figures are standard for an average school in the community. In one scenario, let us assume that the entrepreneur has determined that her new school will cost $900 per student to operate rather than $800 because it needs more staff per student because of specific programmatic goals. If fixed costs remain at $20,000 and no additional revenue is received for the additional programming, this school will need 200 students providing operating margins of $100 each to reach the breakeven point for this school.

Now let us assume that in addition to the higher variable costs per student, the proposed school will have higher fixed costs of $30,000 because of more extensive requirements for its physical space. Since each student provides a contribution margin of $100 toward the fixed costs, the breakeven now rises to 300 students. That is, the $100 margin times 300 students covers the $30,000 fixed costs.

Understanding the behavior of expenses for a given school is clearly important to understanding the potential feasibility of a given school model. Higher variable or fixed expenses may require more students to cover expenses. However, there are other strategies to address this type of scenario. For example, a school that has higher fixed costs may seek grants to cover some of these costs. Variable costs also can be offset with grants, such as state or county funding that is tied directly to students within its districts no matter where they attend school. Examples include textbook subsidies, special education funding, or transportation funding. These funds are based on local and state statutes, so it is important to aggressively investigate what funding is available in a particular area.

Understanding expense behavior can indicate whether a school may need to find ways to reduce variable or fixed expenses if that new school is to succeed. Unfortunately, many school founders plan their new schools as if they will be at full capacity from the very beginning. Usually, it takes several years to build up to full enrollments. Therefore, when modeling the school, it may become necessary to explore numerous scenarios surrounding class size, building size, transportation policies, and so forth to ensure that the school is financially viable during its growth in enrollments.

Often the educational entrepreneur will find that a school can be financially feasible only with very careful budgeting. By understanding the behavior and nature of the various expenses that will be incurred, the entrepreneur can plan for this well in advance of the beginning of operations. Personnel will make up most of the variable expenses for any school. Clear targets can be established for class size. Staffing plans can be tied to specific enrollments to better match revenues with variable expenditures. The ideal class size and the best timing for hiring staff can be determined through a technique known as *sensitivity analysis*. Using this technique, the founder can examine the financial implications of various assumptions regarding class size, salaries, and timing of hiring. By doing so, the school will have a better chance of ensuring that it is financially stable during its start-up. This is discussed in more detail in chapter 8.

When planning to reduce fixed costs, the largest single item is the cost of the school building along with its associated operating expenses. Although it may seem desirable to have a building that a school can grow into over time, the founder must understand that this will create additional cash flow pressures during start-up. Higher fixed costs will mean that the school will need higher enrollments before breakeven cash flow can be achieved. Sometimes it is possible to secure rent concessions if the school commits to a long-term lease. If lower rents can be negotiated for the first year or two, this can dramatically reduce the breakeven enrollment number. Some schools enter into leases for space without ever considering the impact those leases may have on cash flow during the start-up period.

It is important to once again stress that breakeven cash flow should never be the financial goal for a school. For operating purposes alone, it is essential to build up cash reserves as soon as possible. A rule of thumb is that a school should have enough cash reserves to allow for continued operations for at least a month and ideally up to three months, even if revenues are interrupted. If the school depends on public funds, as a charter school might, it is not uncommon for delays around the end of a fiscal year or during government budget crises (not at all an uncommon event). Another contingency that *will* (not *may*) arise for any school is unplanned-for or emergency capital needs. Air conditioners will break, water heaters will burst, or lightning will ruin electronic equipment at some point in time. A reasonable rule of thumb for cash reserves for this need is to keep about 10 percent of the value of fixed assets on hand at all times.

Positive cash flow is also the single most important financial justification for borrowing. Although collateral is considered when borrowing, cash flow is what most concerns bankers who are evaluating loans. A good rule of thumb is to assume that the bank will want to see excess cash flow each month that is two times the amount of the payment on any proposed loan. For example, if the school wants to borrow to buy new computers and plans to make payments over time of $1,000 per month on this loan, the bank may want to see that the school has $2,000 per month in excess cash flow before the loan is approved.

AN EXAMPLE

One of the most common mistakes made by entrepreneurs, whether starting a school or any other type of entity, is failing to recognize inherent fatal flaws in the basic business concept. These flaws are due to market and/or financial causes. The passion that entrepreneurs have for their ideas can blind them to these potential causes of failure. An example of the need for examining market and margin can be found in a nonschool setting from an entrepreneur who came to visit the author several years ago:

[The entrepreneur] was a gifted computer specialist. He came for assistance in getting his cash flow and financing under control. He had identified a market niche for a computer application he had been developing with his previous employer. The employer was not interested in the idea, so the entrepreneur gained permission to take the idea and start his own company to develop and market the product. He had methodically refined the concept and done a remarkable job in making the program operational and ready for market. He reported that he was on the verge of breaking through into the market, but was "dealing with some financial distress." If he could raise a little more money, he would be able to make the business profitable. When asked how bad his financial condition was, he matter-of-factly stated that he had funded his start-up primarily through his life savings (i.e., cashed his retirement accounts) and through a second mortgage on his home. He had gotten "a little behind" on his loan repayment and lost his house. This frustrated his wife, who took their children and left him. And, oh yes, he was about to have his car repossessed. But he only needed to raise another $50,000 and he could deliver his product to several customers. (Cornwall and Naughton 2003, 67)

On further inquiry, the author discovered that this aspiring entrepreneur admitted that he had never really determined the market for the product or the price the customers would pay. In fact, even if he was able to sell to every possible customer in his market, he could generate only about $50,000 in annual revenue. Given that his fixed expenses were over $150,000 before he even paid himself, it was clear that he could never make money on this venture, as he had neither an adequate market nor an adequate margin. Because he was so committed to his idea, he never stopped to consider the most basic aspects of the feasibility of his business. Sadly, many failed school founders can tell similar stories.

SUMMARY

This chapter has explored the first phase of planning for a new school, including the development of a clear, concise, and compelling vision and determining the feasibility of the school idea. The next chapter examines the development of a detailed business plan for the start-up of the school. A business plan includes a complete analysis of and plan for the market, a plan to expand the leadership team, a detailed operating plan, and a financial plan that integrates the findings of the marketing and operating plans into a reliable set of budgets and forecasts.

PART 2

The Planning Phase

CHAPTER 4

The Business Plan

The concept of a *business plan* is foreign to most educators. In fact, the very term can be rather disconcerting to educators because even in a private or charter school setting, they view what they are planning is an educational institution and not a business. But planning for a new school is the same process as planning any new organization. Therefore, a business plan, which has proven to be an invaluable document to most entrepreneurs, also can serve the educational entrepreneur well.

Developing a business plan serves four important purposes:

1. A business plan provides the detailed road map for a new school. The entire start-up team should participate in the development of the business plan if at all possible. This will ensure that the entire team shares a sense of ownership.
2. A business plan can serve as a means of communication about the new project to funding sources for the school. Banks, foundations, government grant agencies, landlords, and major vendors may all be interested in reviewing a business plan before committing to providing financing or funding.
3. A business plan can be used to help recruit people to the start-up team. Administrators, potential board members, business office staff, and lead teachers may be easier to attract with a clear and compelling plan.
4. A business plan can help point out serious problems with the project before a large amount of resources are committed. As in the feasibility assessment discussed in chapter 3, some problems in

the project plan can be proactively pursued and corrected in the planning stage. Others may be fatal flaws that indicate that the project should be terminated even before it begins. Just as is the case in the feasibility assessment, the goal is "to fail on paper" rather than to fail after operations have commenced.

This chapter presents a model for creating a business plan that will help guide the development and implementation of new entrepreneurial education initiatives and improve their chances for success. To be effectively developed, a business plan cannot be written by simply following an outline, such as that that at the end of the chapter, step-by-step. Rather, it should be developed following a logical order that ensures that the plan will have internal consistency and a greater probability of presenting what actually may happen in the start-up school. If fundamental inconsistencies arise, the project should be changed or abandoned, depending on the nature of the inconsistency. This chapter is intended as a road map for developing a more effective business plan. Such an overview is critical to understanding the interrelationships of the various components of planning a new school start-up, and it is important to keep in mind the basic internal logic that should guide the entire plan.

STEP 1: MISSION AND RATIONALE

The planning process should begin with a clear statement of purpose. As discussed in chapter 2, this statement of purpose will come out of the leaders' vision for the project. For the purposes of the business plan, the vision should be communicated through the mission statement, which should 1) be a clear statement of what the educational venture is going to be, 2) define who it is intended to serve, and 3) identify where it is going to operate. The mission statement takes the vision of the founding leadership team and brings it into the here and now.

The *rationale* for a new project describes the source of the opportunity. It presents the external factors that created the need for the project, including trends, facts, and data taken from local, regional, and national perspectives. This information should have been developed during the first stage of the start-up process described in the previous chapter.

In the example of the St. Paul charter school for Hispanic youth, supporting rationale came from a variety of sources. A sample of the information that supported the development of the school included a growth in the Latino population in St. Paul, local and state support for new charter schools, an increasing number of willing sponsors for charter schools, and strong demand for additional educational services focusing on the Latino community in St. Paul.

A summary of all critical information should be incorporated to build support for the opportunity. Chapter 5 discusses a variety of issues that need to be addressed when presenting the general market conditions for a new school. What are the underlying trends that support this new school? What others schools will be competing for the same students? What are the characteristics of the local environment for this school? Depending on the audience, the rationale section of the plan may actually be fairly short. If the audience is very familiar with the rationale for the new school, a tightly written summary of up to two pages should suffice. The information should still be included, however, as it will serve as a reminder of the school's rationale and purpose to all involved. There will almost certainly come a time in the near future when the team will need to revisit their reasons for working so hard and taking such risks. If other stakeholders, such as funders, are going to read the plan, a somewhat longer version of the rationale with a little more detail or explanation would be justified, but the presentation should still be kept to no more than roughly five pages.

STEP 2: MARKETING PLAN

Marketing is a negative term to some in the field of education. It conjures up images of slick messages used at the expense of the actual quality of educational services. Controversies over corporate sponsorships in schools have only fueled this perception. To some, it represents a cheapening of education, turning parents and children into customers and education into a commodity.

However, marketing is simply a tool. And it is a tool that is being used effectively by the growing number of private and semipublic educational systems competing with each other and with public school systems for enrollment. Marketing, as discussed in more detail in chapter 6, is actually a collection of several important functions that any organization does, some more effectively and consciously than others. A key function of marketing is educating the public about an organization and its products or services. Schools do this all the time with newsletters, roadside information signs, fliers, phone book ads, news releases, and so forth. As all schools begin to compete more and more for students, this communication function of marketing becomes increasingly essential. While competition may be a distasteful notion to many in the education field, it has become a reality in recent years. To successfully compete in this arena, schools must develop the capacity to engage in the communication function of marketing. However, marketing involves several additional functions, including pricing, the array of services being offered by the school, and even the media that are used to disseminate knowledge (such as the Internet as a learning medium).

STEP 3: REVENUE PLAN

In an operating school, much of what is known about available revenues from year to year is derived from the traditional budgeting process that is based on past years' history. However, a new school has no history, so an alternative method for estimating revenues is required. (Note that expenses are not developed in detail until step 5.) Even after a new school is opened, revenues should not be derived from the first year's figures. Doing so would not yield good predictions because of the continual changes in the school's enrollment.

Many entrepreneurs (of all types) make a critical and often disastrous mistake at this point in their planning. Our training in traditional budgeting teaches us to spend most of our time estimating expenses that will be required to run the organization. In fact, it has been demonstrated that, left to their own, most entrepreneurs will spend at least 80 percent of the time massaging and modeling the various categories of expenses and less than 20 percent of the time estimating revenues. In fact, many entrepreneurs will simply estimate revenues on the basis of the expenses they anticipate spending. However, accuracy in revenue forecasting is what most often makes or breaks an entrepreneurial venture of any type. If one assumes a level of revenues on the basis of very little systematic thought and then makes commitments for spending on the basis of those revenue projections, disaster can occur if those revenue estimates do not materialize.

Constructing revenue forecasts for a new initiative should begin with the information developed in the marketing plan, which is discussed in the next two chapters. By looking at the structure of the market, combined with the plan to attract families to the new school, a realistic revenue forecast can be determined. Forecasts should be made for several time periods into the future (at least three years and preferably five) to accurately model anticipated growth in enrollments over time. To develop accurate forecasts of revenues, many entrepreneurs find that they spend 80 percent of their time on *revenue estimates* and only 20 percent estimating expenses.

Another key component of forecasting is to create an inventory of the major assumptions used to make the revenue forecasts. Assumptions need to be made when establishing forecasts. Each time a major assumption is made, it should be documented. The list of assumptions will then help serve as a control mechanism as the initiative develops. The leaders should frequently test the assumptions that were made. If key assumptions were not correct, the forecasts should be immediately adjusted to determine the potential financial impact so that any necessary corrective actions can be made quickly and decisively. For example, the model for a new charter school may assume a certain level of funding per pupil and a certain class size. If the funding level turns out to be less than anticipated because of the ever-changing state political climate, then expenses may need to be adjusted to reflect the decrease in actual revenues versus those forecasted. On the other hand, if the leadership observes that the new school can support larger class sizes than was originally assumed, previously cut expenses may be able to be restored because of higher revenues. This demonstrates why leading a start-up educational venture requires a management style that is both highly focused (a tight watch on the key assumptions) and flexible (readily adaptable to changing conditions).

The final component of the financial plan is the list of key milestones and measures of success during start-up and growth. For each key milestone, such as opening day or the end of the first term, predetermined measures for success up to that point should be evaluated. In addition to monitoring assumptions, measures of success at key milestones will be the other primary tool to allow for "midcourse corrections" for the new school. Chapter 9 examines in greater detail the development and use of assumptions and financial milestones.

STEP 4: OPERATING AND TEAM PLANS

Most school administrators with experience in traditional public schools are well trained in the development of operating plans, which is the next step in the development of the business plan. A detailed description of all space and resource needs should be included. Resources might include special computer software and hardware, special equipment, and unusual library resources in addition to any standard equipment needs. However, developing an operating plan for a freestanding, financially independent new school may require a whole new approach to planning the operations of the school. Creative methods of making the most of scarce financial resources are a standard requirement for most school start-ups. Using a variety of tools and techniques developed by experienced entrepreneurs facing financial dire straits is known collectively as *bootstrapping*. There are a wide variety of bootstrapping techniques and tools, and these discussed in full in chapter 9.

Part of the operating plan includes the development of policies and procedures. Certainly, established policies and procedures from existing schools in the system can serve as a starting point. However, this portion of the operating plan should be tailored to fit the specific nature of any new school and, most important, the culture that the leadership wishes to instill within the new school. Therefore, each policy and procedure should be carefully measured against the vision and desired culture of the school that the founder envisions creating.

Specific plans for organizational structure should be outlined in this portion of the business plan. How are basic functions going to be organized, and who will supervise these functions? For example, in many private schools today, child care programs are common. Will one curriculum manager oversee both parts of the school, or will there be separate management of these two components? Such decisions will have structural, budgetary, and cultural implications that must all be carefully considered and evaluated.

Specific governance plans should be described. Who will make up the governing board, and how will the initial members be recruited and approved? For example, some states have regulations requiring teacher representation on charter school boards. However, during the planning stage, no teachers may yet be under contract to the school. Therefore, a plan must address the founding board and any transition that will need to take place to an ongoing operating board. Plans to train and orient board members should be included, and any budgetary items associated with this should be represented in the financial forecasts.

Staffing plans will need to be carefully tied to anticipated patterns of growth established in the revenue forecast model and the marketing plan. Staffing plans should also reflect the desired culture and vision of the initiative under plan. Growth in teaching, support, and administrative staff should all be tied to specific revenue and size targets. These targets should be points at which increased revenues can in fact cover the new staff expense. Communication about the staffing plan is important, especially because existing staff may feel somewhat stretched until more staff can be added. Assurance that help will be coming at a specific juncture should reduce the distress caused by these growing pains.

A specific component of the staffing plan examines the needs for an expanding leadership team as the school grows. The team plan (examined in detail in chapter 7) should have two basic components. First, it should include a brief description of known team members, including their role and qualifications, and a description of any specific team members who will need to be added for the start-up. Second, the team plan should include a team development plan. The team plan should include any transition plans anticipated for the leadership of the new project over time. It is not unusual for founding members of the leadership team to transition to other opportunities over time. Many people drawn to start-ups grow restless as an organization begins to mature and stabilize, eventually choosing to pursue other start-up ventures.

STEP 5: EXPENSE PLAN

At this point in the development of the business plan, the leadership team should return to the financial plan to create the detail of the expense portion of their forecasts. Expenses should be forecast for three to five years to correspond to the revenue forecasts that were already established in step 3. The fully developed marketing and operating plans can provide much of the detail. Recall what was stated previously: Only about 20 percent of business planning time should be allocated to creating expense forecasts. Experienced educators should be able to create accurate expense forecasts in a relatively short period of time. Expense forecasts used in the business plan should *not* be used without further revision before being used for budgetary purposes. Actual budgeting should be a separate process tied to traditional financial control systems. Start-ups should not be tightly managed by each expense category even in the budgetary system. Budget review should take into account the uncertainty of such a project and allow for flexibility in creating a balanced budget overall. Expenses in the budget should not be considered a commitment to spend, as is true in public schools. Chapter 9 examines the budgetary process in start-ups in detail.

If the revenue forecasts developed in step 3 do not result in a balanced budget in the business plan, the expenses should be adjusted first, not the revenue forecasts. Do not "plug" the revenue forecasts to fit anticipated spending; that is, never simply make the budget balance by putting in ("plugging") a revenue estimate that will cover the estimated expenses. If adjusting expenses does not achieve acceptable financial outcomes, then all assumptions should be reviewed to see whether there are any adjustments in the basic framework of the school itself. For example, assumptions on class size, qualification level of staff, use of teacher aides, number and role of administrative staff, definition of market, and so on may need to be challenged to determine whether changes can result in a balanced budget while still meeting the basic mission of the school.

This point in planning creates a crucial "go/no go" point. If the forecasts cannot support the financial viability of the new school, the idea may need to be abandoned before any more resources are committed. If there is no margin, there is no mission, and failure on paper is preferable to the failure of a start-up.

STEP 6: WRITING THE BUSINESS PLAN

All the information gathered up to this point can now be pulled together into the business plan. As stated at the beginning of this chapter, the plan is not developed in the same order that it is finally presented. Once all the key sections have been developed using the process outlined thus far, it can be assembled into a standard business plan format. By following the steps in order, the plan should have strong internal consistency and will provide a strong presentation while also serving as a valuable guide for the start-up process. The marketing plan will tie clearly into and inform the revenue forecasts. The expense forecasts are clearly explained by the details presented in the operating plan.

The final version of the business plan will present the information in an order that will flow most logically for the reader. The specific organization of business plans can vary significantly. Most follow an outline starting with the factors that explain the opportunity for the new venture. This is followed by an examination of how the new school will seize this opportunity and operate in a financially sound manner. One variant on this approach is when the founding team is well-known and may be one of the primary reasons that a school will attract external support, especially financial support. Financial backing can be based, in part, on who is actually leading or supporting the leadership of the school. In private entrepreneurial ventures, this is known as *investing in the people* rather than investing in the specific idea. The leaders have a track record of success and are expected to continue this performance in any new initiative they intend to pursue. In this case, the outline of the plan may include a detailed discussion of the team members, their past track record, and their past accomplishments as one of the very first sections of the plan. Another variation may be dictated by funding sources. For example, it is traditional to put detailed financial information toward the end of the business plan. However, a funding source may require that information at the beginning of the plan. It is important to gain an understanding of any requirements such as this in advance.

It may be necessary to write more than one version of the business plan. It is common for funding sources to require a format that includes limited information on the marketing and operations plan, expanded information on the mission and leadership team, and much of the remaining focus on the financial statements. The leadership team should have a comprehensive version of the plan that includes all the details discussed in this section of the book. A third version of the plan may be developed for teachers. This would have limited information on the market and financial targets but full detail on the mission and operating plan. Even a fourth version may be developed for parents. This would have limited detail on all sections except the mission and vision for the school.

A suggested outline for a comprehensive business plan is as follows:

1. *Executive summary:* Provides a complete synopsis of the project (discussed in the final step of the planning process that follows this outline).
2. *Mission of the project:* Clearly states the purpose of the project, where it will be delivered, and whom it will serve; also includes a description of the desired organizational culture.
3. *Rationale:* Presents the external factors that are the source for the opportunity and should include trends, facts, and data taken from local, regional, and national perspectives.
4. *Marketing plan:* Includes an analysis of the competition, the results of market research, a description of how the project will fit in the market, and a promotional plan.
5. *Operating plan:* Includes consideration of space and staffing needs; also presents basic information on how the project will be managed.
6. *The team:* Usually presented in a separate section. It should list known members of the start-up team and descriptions of the type of people who will need to be added to the team. A maximum of one page should be dedicated to the team. However, it may be advisable to include résumés of the founders as an appendix.
7. *Financial plan:* Displays financial projections and the assumptions used to create those projections. For nonprofit schools, cash flow statements (statements of operations based on cash flow) are the minimum requirement. However, the inclusion of balance sheets also may be advisable. For-profit schools should include income statements, statements of cash flows, and balance sheets. Financial projections for the first five years are fairly standard. The first two to three years should include month-by-month detail in any description of cash flow.

STEP 7: EXECUTIVE SUMMARY

The final step in developing the business plan is to write an executive summary. The executive summary serves as an overview of the entire plan that can communicate its essence within one or, at most, two pages. It is not simply an introduction to the business plan that grabs the readers' attention so that they read the whole plan. Instead, it should capture all the main points and conclusions from the plan in a single page. The executive summary will serve as an important communication tool for the initiative with internal and external constituencies.

SUMMARY

This chapter has presented outlines for both the process of creating a business plan for a new school and for presenting the actual business plan itself. Subsequent chapters provide detail on each major component of the plan. Chapters 5 and 6 examine the development of the marketing plan, chapters 7 and 8 focus on the operating aspects of the new school, and chapter 9 provides details on the financial planning for the start-up process.

CHAPTER 5

Understanding the Market

Schools today operate within active and changing markets. School choice has created a variety of options for families to evaluate for educating their children. The ability of any new school to successfully enter into the market requires a clear understanding of that market. This includes general market conditions and the competitive environment. Understanding the market requires the accumulation and analysis of a variety of data. This chapter examines the process of gaining an understanding of a new school's market through systematic research and evaluation of data.

MARKET RESEARCH

Market research is the systematic approach to gathering data about the general market conditions, the competitive environment, and the customers of an organization in a format that will assist the leadership team in making better decisions. The first step in market research is to clearly define what the entrepreneur needs to learn more about. The following sections present a variety of questions that will need to be researched.

Once a preliminary list of research questions has been created (it is only preliminary, as questions will continuously arise that require ongoing research and assessment), the entrepreneur will have to determine the best approach to gathering information to answer these questions. Different questions will require different sources for gathering information. Two basic categories of data sources can be used for market research: primary or secondary. *Primary data* consist of information that is directly gathered from the source. For example, the entrepreneur may decide to gather information directly from potential customers. *Secondary data* consist of information that has already been gathered by someone else and is available to others as either raw information or summarized statistics. In this case, the entrepreneur may use published reports that provide summary statistical data on the potential customer group that the school will be serving. Within each category of data source, a variety of specific data-gathering strategies can be utilized.

There are two general strategies for gathering primary data. Formal primary data consists of information that is systematically collected from customers or other key groups. There are specific steps that guide the gathering of formal primary data:

1. *Design data-collection instrument:* Data can be gathered using an interview guide or a questionnaire. Interview guides are most often used to gather data in face-to-face meetings or via telephone interviews. Questionnaires ask the respondents to answer questions themselves. Questionnaires can be administered through mail surveys, via the Internet, using "captured audiences" (such as attendees at a conference), through insertion in newsletters, and so forth. Most instruments will gather basic demographic data that are pertinent to what is being studied, such as age, income, and ethnicity, as well as a variety of preference questions related to the primary focus of the study, in this case the new school. It may ask questions regarding curriculum, focus or theme, inclusion of extra- and cocurricular activities, food service, transportation, fees and tuition, and other relevant topics. It also is common to gather data on competitive schools or alternative methods of education, such as home schooling. Thus, a well-constructed instrument will help answer key questions regarding general market conditions, competitive schools, and preferences regarding key features of the new school.

2. *Test the instrument:* Such a test should be performed on a small subsample to make sure the instrument is understandable and measures what is intended by each item. Even instruments designed by experienced researchers will undergo some refinement

during testing, so this is a step that should not be bypassed. If a test is not performed, some items on the instrument may result in less-than-perfect data or even useless information.

3. *Collect data from a sample of the population or, if small enough, the entire population being studied:* A sample makes for a less expensive study without much of a loss in accuracy. However, care must be taken to ensure that the sample is representative of the population (random samples are the most common method to achieve this outcome).

4. *Analyze the data to gain an understanding of the population being studied:* It is important to restate the key questions the entrepreneur needs to learn about so that the results can be summarized in a useful format for decision making.

Three important factors may lead an entrepreneur to forgo any formal primary research. First, the cost of formal primary market research can be too high for many entrepreneurs on a tight budget. Good primary research can cost thousands of dollars by the time the instrument is designed and tested and the data are gathered and analyzed. Sometimes it is possible to have such research conducted at a much lower cost using graduate or undergraduate students from a local university to perform part or all of the study as a part of their course work. Second, time may be a reason not to use formal primary research. Such studies can take several months to conduct from start to finish. Time is often a constraint for entrepreneurs, especially if start-up is tied to a particular time of year, as is the case with new schools. Third, depending on the questions that need to be answered, the entrepreneur may be able to get data that are almost as accurate at a fraction of the time and cost of a formal research study using other strategies.

Many entrepreneurs are able to successfully rely on what is known as *informal primary data*, which are collected anecdotally from potential customers and other key constituencies. For example, an entrepreneur starting a residential school for mentally ill teenagers was able to gain thorough and accurate data by meeting with a few of the key potential referral sources and funders of the proposed school. Since the number of funders and referral sources was fairly small and they controlled a large segment of this market, the information proved to be both accurate and highly informative for the planning of the new residential school. One feature that had not been part of the original plans that proved to be critical to both groups was a strong transition program to help children successfully return to their communities. In the case of a new Catholic school, the planners met over several evenings with parent groups from the market area to determine the level of interest and any key concerns these parents had in common. Again, such data proved to be easily, inexpensively, and quickly gathered and turned out to be an accurate predictor of the market conditions this school would face as it began operations. Even though informal primary data are generally much less expensive and easier to gather, such data may prove to be unreliable because of data collection biases. Care must be taken to ensure that the research is not designed just to find out what the entrepreneurs want to hear in the first place, such as that the school is a good idea. It is important to recognize the potential bias of such data and consequently make every effort to gain accurate and critical data.

Secondary data also can be useful in the planning stages of a new school, even if primary data have already been gathered. The most common sources of secondary data include a wide variety of studies conducted by various government agencies (federal, state, and local). Such data often are available in detail in government reports or summarized in published articles. Internet research can prove to be a rich source of information, as most agencies publish their data on-line at no cost to the user. Secondary data are also available from educationally focused groups. For example, a great deal of information is available on charter schools from groups that support the development of these schools. Various foundations publish reports on alternative forms of education that are consistent with their missions. Secondary data can prove to be a good source on average operating costs, enrollment patterns, and funding sources.

Finally, once all the data have been gathered, the entrepreneur begins to summarize the results and incorporate the significant conclusions into the marketing plan. Such information can provide strong, credible support for the intuitive understanding of the opportunity already developed by the entrepreneur. It can help solidify the entrepreneur's understanding of the market and point out the probable success of various strategies and tactics discussed in the marketing plan. Even though the entrepreneur may already have strong knowledge and expertise about these issues, supporting such knowledge and expertise with data adds credibility.

GENERAL MARKET CONDITIONS

The first set of issues that require careful consideration in the planning process are the various factors that make up the general market conditions in which the school will operate. This includes factors shaping the societal, economic, political, regulatory, and demographic environment in which the school will exist. Some of these operate at the national level, while others are more local.

Several key questions must be considered in order to understand these general market conditions. These questions will help shape the entrepreneur's understanding of the market in ways that are necessary to successfully compete. What general forces or trends will help create the market for this school? Are they related to society, the economy, politics, demographics, or some combination of these forces? Is this school based on an idea that works in another market or even a similar idea that works in another setting? Are there more specific changes in regulations or funding that will support the new school? Key market forces should be documented and integrated into almost any version of a business plan. It is important for the leadership team, staff, outside funders, and conceivably even parents to understand what forces support the creation of the new school. Key trends should be carefully researched and thoroughly understood. Such information will include both objective facts and figures as well as subjective analysis of general trends and market forces.

General forces and trends that relate to the school should be consistent with the vision for the new school that was articulated in the beginning of the business plan. The vision should make sense in light of the general market conditions the school will be facing. For example, if the vision is to create a school for a specific demographic group, the general market conditions should show that there will be an adequate population and positive trends that will support this school into the future. The new Catholic school and the Latino charter school discussed in chapters 2 and 3 are good examples of entities with visions that were consistent with the general market trends in their communities.

Examination of market conditions should not be a one-time event conducted before the start-up planning for the new school. Evaluation of general market conditions should be an ongoing process that becomes an integral part of planning and decision making throughout the life of the school. Leaders should continue to ask critical questions about the general market conditions for their school. Have the conditions changed that created the original opportunity for the school? If so, how do these changes affect the school in the future? What trends need to be tracked in the future about the market and the industry that can adversely affect the basic opportunity that supported the formation of the school? These questions should be carefully and honestly evaluated on a regular basis (at a minimum, annually). School founders should develop a short list of key trends, methods of tracking these trends, and a plan to collect and reflect on information gathered.

Specific responsibility to collect information on market conditions should be assigned to all members of the leadership team. Each may have access to different data related to specific roles in the management of the school. For example, one of the leaders may have more contact with state officials, one with the local school district, and another with a key national association. Each perspective is critical to understand the overall environment for the school. Typically, evaluating this information should be a primary function of annual planning meetings.

COMPETITIVE ANALYSIS

The first step in creating an effective marketing plan is to gain a thorough understanding of "the competition." The concept of competing for students may seem foreign to most educators who have spent their careers in public K–12 school settings. However, it is anything but foreign to educators in colleges and universities. Competition for college and graduate students has grown fierce in recent years, thereby creating a whole new way of thinking about attracting students through traditional business marketing strategies. The same is beginning to occur in the increasingly competitive environment of K–12 education.

Understanding the competitive environment a school faces will go a long way toward shaping and developing the marketing strategies it will use. Marketing strategies include an array of decisions on the nature of services to be offered, pricing, the location and medium of educational delivery, and how the school will be promoted to potential students and their families. These concepts are discussed in more detail in the next chapter.

A complete analysis of the competitive environment requires accurate market research. To compete effectively, a new school must have accurate data regarding the most important criteria on which parents base their school decision.

Primary market research on customers is generally conducted through surveys, interviews, or focus groups. Surveys are structured questionnaires that are administered to potential customers. Once the surveys are returned, the information is summarized to try and capture the thinking of the families who will be potential customers. Surveys work best if they are kept fairly short, usually one to two pages maximum, and have easy-to-mark responses. The advantage of a survey is that if enough people respond, this method can give a fairly accurate view of the entire population of people being studied—in this case, potential customers—in regard to their general opinions and preferences. One disadvantage of surveys is their relatively high cost. Printing, distribution, tabulation, and analysis can often run hundreds and even thousands of dollars. Another disadvantage is that surveys usually give overly simplified responses. There is little opportunity to explain opinions and no chance to capture information that is not built into the questions in the survey. Critical data can be missed because a question is not asked in the survey. Yet another disadvantage is that the response rate on mail surveys is historically low (can be less than 10 percent), making such data difficult to analyze with any confidence.

Interviews can allow for a richer source of information. Potential families can answer in their own words and provide explanations for their responses. Interviews can use more open-ended questions that allow the respondents to answer without the limitations imposed by the forced-choice format of a survey. One risk with using interviews is that they may not be representative of the entire population's opinions. It is crucial to interview a number of people with varying opinions and with varying degrees of interest in the new school. It also may be difficult to summarize the results of the interviews accurately. A predetermined method of tabulating the responses should be developed and followed carefully. Interviews are generally much cheaper to administer than surveys and therefore are the most common method used by entrepreneurs in any type of setting.

The use of focus groups draws on some of the advantages of both surveys and interviews. Generally, focus groups work best if conducted by a trained, experienced leader. If done properly, focus groups can provide more accurate and representative data that are also richer in content than survey data. However, just as with surveys, focus groups can be expensive, especially for a start-up organization on a very limited budget.

Whichever method is used, the market research should answer three fundamental questions.

1. *Who is most likely to choose our school?* To help answer this question, it is important to gather basic demographic data about the respondents, which may include address, socioeconomic status, education level of parents, religious affiliation (for religious schools), employment, and so forth. Once the data are gathered, the demographic data and the opinion data should be used together to determine the general characteristics of those families most likely to choose the new school for their children. For example, market research may find that middle- to upper-class families with parents who attended college are most likely to consider sending their children to the new school. Or it may be Hmong families within a one-mile radius of the school site. Or it may be families who belong to more fundamentalist-leaning churches. Clearly, the market research must communicate at some point the vision and mission of the new school. This information should be used to assess generalized opinions and preferences about the proposed vision and mission. Research may yield some unexpected findings. The potential market may be much smaller or much larger than first thought, or it may look different than originally anticipated. For example,

many religiously based schools find a surprising number of families not affiliated with a specific faith being drawn to the school. The basic values and vision may simply resonate with these families regardless of the differences in faith. A goal of any market research should be to challenge preconceived ideas about who may be the real potential customers of the new school.

2. *What criteria do these families use in choosing a school for their children?* The market research may find that of those customers most likely to choose the new school, safety, college admission success, discipline, and accessibility of teachers to students and parents are rated the most important criteria in their choice of a school. The relative ranking of these criteria is important to ascertain when attempting to answer this question.

3. *How do these families rate our competitors on these criteria?* Market research should assess which schools are the strongest competitors for the new school in their decision-making process and how well each of these is rated on the key criteria. When assessing the competition, it is critical not to overlook possible educational alternatives (such as home schooling or Internet education). Again, the goal is to objectively evaluate the competitive position of the new school even before it opens its doors. For example, a charter school that targets a specific ethnic community may be surprised by the loyalty that many of their targeted customers already have for the public school in their community. Such a finding may dramatically change how or even whether this new school plans to open.

The best way to organize all of these data for decision making and planning is to use what is known as a *competitive analysis matrix*. An example is displayed in table 5.1. The first step in creating a competitive analysis matrix is to list all competitors along the left side of the grid. This should include those competitors identified by potential customers and any others that the school founders believe will compete for students. This list should also include options such as home schooling.

The first column on the top of the figure identifies the market share of each competitor. For schools, market share is measured with enrollments.

Table 5.1. Sample Competitive Analysis Matrix for a Proposed New Private High School

	Enrollment	Safety	College Prep	Sports	Access to Teachers
Public high school	1,500	School has two full-time police officers on duty 20 significant incidents in past year with reported violence and/or weapons General perception in community is that school had significant problems in the past but that the school has become much safer in past two years	70% of graduates are admitted to schools of higher education 20% of these students received academic scholarship offers	Full range of boys' and girls' sports Seven state titles in past five years Participation rate is less than 10% of students	Perceived to be improving with new e-mail system in place
Local Catholic school	400	General perception in community is that school is very safe with any incidents as being a rare occurrence	90% of graduates are admitted to schools of higher education 60% of these students received academic scholarship offers	All major sports except football and hockey Perceived as competitive in their conference in most sports Fairly open to most students	Excellent access reported Teachers reported as working very closely with students

	Enrollment	Safety	College Prep	Sports	Access to Teachers
Existing charter school with science and math focus	210	General perception in community is that school is very safe, although it is located in a relatively dangerous neighborhood	98% of graduates are admitted to schools of higher education 80% of these students received academic scholarship offers	None; students can try out for sports at the public high school	Excellent access reported Teachers reported as working very closely with students, including collaboration on research projects
Home schooling	Approximately 50	n/a	Anecdotal evidence is that almost all these students go on to higher education	None	Excellent network of specialized tutors in the community are widely used by this group
Our proposed new school	Estimated 240	School will be located in a safe neighborhood Strict code of conduct will be developed and enforced	Goal is to have 100% of graduates go on to college	Club sports planned in soccer, basketball, and lacrosse	Expectation is that all faculty will have office hours daily They will communicate frequently (at least every other week and more if problems arise) via e-mail or phone with parents on student progress

The remaining columns list all the key customer decision-making criteria. Once the basic grid is completed, each school should be evaluated for each criterion and those results entered into the cells of the matrix. The rating should be as specific as possible, avoiding generalized ratings such as "good" or "fair."

Only customer perceptions or other objective data should go in the cells of the grid, not your own opinions. The goal is not to find flaws with competitors and unrealistically build up the prospects for the new school. Rather, the evaluation should be as accurate, truthful, and objective as possible. As is seen in table 5.1, the evaluation should be complete enough to establish clear and explicit differentiation among the schools included in the matrix.

In addition to the traditional forms of market research discussed thus far, the founders should gather some additional data for the competitive analysis. For example, if at all possible, the school leaders should visit their competitors. Through such visits, the generalized perceptions gathered through the market research can be verified. More generalized perceptions can be enhanced by direct observation. While it may be tempting to pretend to be prospective parents when visiting, there clearly are serious ethical issues with such an approach. Deception is never advisable. Surprisingly, many schools will welcome others into the market. In fact, several charter schools in Minnesota have board members who are leaders of other schools, including other charter schools that may potentially compete for students. Most schools went through their own start-ups and remember how much they relied on the help they received from established schools in the community.

Once completed, the competitive analysis matrix should remain a part of all major planning and decision making. It should be updated each year to make sure that the information on the competitors, the customers' decision-making criteria, and the evaluations are accurate. The matrix is an important part of the business plan for a new school and should be included in any ongoing strategic plans that the school may compile in the future.

MARKET SEGMENTATION AND MARKET POSITIONING

As noted in the previous section, the criteria for choosing a school vary between families even within the same market. For the educational entrepreneur, this is good. Variation in preferences creates an opportunity to serve those families who are not currently being served by existing schools. That is what was previously referred to as a market niche. Most businesses focus on one customer group, as it is often difficult to be all things to all customers. This is called *market segmentation.* Segmentation allows businesses to serve the needs of common group or groups of customers. General research into the most common bases of market segmentation used by small businesses fits well with school start-ups and what determines their market segments. The following is a list of those general bases (in order of most common use):

By demographic group, including religion, ethnic group, and language

By geographic area, including neighborhood, community, city, and county

By benefits sought, based on what the customer wants, for example, convenience and safety, reputation, or academic challenge

The process of identifying the best fit within the various market segments is called *market positioning.* Not every school can serve every family. Therefore, the school should determine which segment of the market it can best serve given the constraints it faces (such as facilities, mission, budget, and statutory limitations). Public school systems typically have tried to serve the market as if it is homogeneous in its needs. However, markets are diverse and may require different services for the different segments. The business plan should include an accurate assessment of the total size of the market and of each segment within that market. Clearly, many charter schools have been started as the result of segments of the population that believe that traditional public schools, as they have been historically operated, do not meet the criteria that are important for these parents in their school choice.

In some instances, it may be necessary to identify the various diverse segments of the local market that share common preferences in schools and then perform a competitive analysis for each to see exactly where a new school fits in this diverse market. For example, one charter school was established to serve a particular immigrant group. However, in planning, the founders realized that a second segment of the market—families who wanted their children immersed in another culture and language—proved to be rather significant and enthusiastic about the charter school. The school established a market position that served both these market segments, and enrollments proved to be even more robust than originally planned. Once a decision is made regarding the segments of the market, competitive strategies should be developed for each segment (see chapter 4). All this should then be included in the business plan.

Obviously, 100 percent market share (that is, all possible students in the market) is unrealistic and, in fact, impossible. However, it is essential to develop an accurate estimate of enrollments, as that is what will drive the revenue forecasts in the budget (see chapter 9). The first step is to create an estimate of the total size of the market and of each market segment (total number of potential students). This figure can be derived from available public data sources and the market research of potential customers.

In looking at the competitive analysis matrix in table 5.1, it can be determined that this market has total of 2,400 high school students. Assume that market research determined that the estimated size of the market segment that would be attracted to the new proposed school was about 20 percent of the total population. That means that the size of the total market segment for our school is 480. Next, a realistic goal for market share (percentage of market segment or total market) can be determined. Our main competitive factor—safety and discipline—is not the only criteria that families evaluate. The other factors will also come into the decision-making process. In addition, specific factors, such as friendships in existing schools, will limit how many students can be attracted. We believe that because of the strength of the positive responses in our market research, we can expect to enroll at least half of these 480 students. A forecast for enrollments is then calculated by taking market share times total market for each segment. That is where our estimate of 240 in the matrix comes from. It is a number that is systematically derived, not just someone's "best guess."

In a start-up, it is wise to assume that full enrollment (in our example, 240 students) will not be attained during the first year unless there are compelling data to indicate that such enrollments are possible. A three-year ramp-up to maximum projected enrollments is not an unrealistic assumption for growth.

SUMMARY

Determining market segment and market positioning is the critical first step in developing a marketing strategy. The next chapter continues this discussion by using this information to make decisions on services, pricing, location and mediums of delivery, and promotion for a new school project. We return to the processes discussed in this chapter when the link between marketing plans and revenue forecasts in the business plan is discussed in chapter 9.

CHAPTER 6

The Marketing Plan

Effective marketing requires that entrepreneurs truly know their customers. Much has already been learned about customers as entrepreneurs gain a better understanding of their markets (see chapter 5). With this knowledge, entrepreneurs are better able to communicate with their customers and more effectively manage their customer relationships.

The fundamental goal of the *marketing plan* is to develop a systematic set of activities to help a school effectively engage and communicate with its customers. Effective communication is always a two-way process. Thus, the marketing plan addresses not only how to communicate *with* the school's customers but also how to facilitate the customers in effective communication with the school. In both cases, the communication is as often indirect as it is direct. For example, the school creates a direct message to its customers in the text included in a brochure. However, that same brochure contains many indirect messages as well. The photographs, font, colors, and paper quality all add to the message.

A vernacular definition of what marketing entails is usually limited to selling and/or advertising. In fact, marketing is often viewed as a little unseemly for some types of organizations (health care, law, and schools). However, communicating with customers includes much more than selling and advertising. Messages to the customers also are created through pricing strategies and policies, services offered, and even the physical location of the school itself. That is why marketing is known as the "four Ps":

Product: Making sure the school offers the customer the services that they need and want

Pricing: What and how the school charges the customer for its various services

Place (location or distribution): Where and how the school gets its product to the customer

Promotion: How the school communicates with its customers about its product

Taken together, these are known as the *marketing mix.* Therefore, the marketing plan defines how the school will engage and communicate with its customers through its marketing mix.

PRODUCT

Offering the right set of educational services for the marketplace is the goal of this part of the marketing mix. Too often, entrepreneurs view the planning for this to be only a part of preparation for start-up. However, few businesses or nonprofits operate in an environment that never changes. The very elements of the marketplace that created the opportunity are in a constant state of evolution or even revolution. Savvy competitors constantly update the products or services they offer. Therefore, to survive over the long run, entrepreneurs must be prepared to adjust, refine, repair, or even reinvent what they offer to their customers to at least keep up with change and at best to become part of the market leadership of change.

Even though schools offer a service, the same principles apply as to any business that offers a product. Those trained in education typically view the definition of the "product" they offer quite narrowly. Product, if it is considered at all, is thought of in terms of the education that is delivered to the students in the classroom. In fact, product includes everything that incorporates the experience of gaining an education in a school. *Product* for a school system includes not only curriculum offerings but also all the other criteria that parents use in making a choice of schools. This can include quality and experience of the faculty, extracurricular options, the school's reputation for placement in higher education, safety, child care, food service, facilities, and so forth. Managing the product of a school requires that all that goes into the school experience be understood from the customer's perspective.

A recent visit to a junior high school is a case in point. The school presents itself as a community that includes staff, students, and parents. This, in effect, defines its product as a public school. In public introductions to new parents, the importance of parental involvement in the school is espoused as a fundamental aspect of what the school is "all about." Brochures and other materials state that it is a school that is "fueled by parental volunteerism." However, parents tell a different story. They say that when they arrive at the front office to report in for volunteer activities, they are treated with indifference or even ignored by the staff. When parents finally make their way to the classroom, many of the teachers show little gratitude and even marginalize the parental volunteers. Clearly, what the principal describes as the school's product and how it is experienced by its customers are in stark contrast. Actions and not simply words are what define a school's product.

A different example can be found in a residential school for troubled teenage boys. The director of the school believed in his own mind that the behavior management and classroom components of the school were the only essential components of his product. If he got that right, nothing else really mattered. However, to the parents, the product they were interested in included professionalism of the staff, food quality, cleanliness, and their perception of safety protocol as critically important parts of the product. The director failed to grasp what the true nature of his product really was *in the minds of his customers.*

To effectively manage this product, a school leader will need to decide on all four of the factors that make up a service business:

1. *Extensiveness of services:* This gets to the heart of the issues discussed thus far regarding the product of the school. What is the range of services to be provided by the school?
2. *Degree of involvement by the customer:* An example of this in a service business would be a full-service restaurant versus cafeteria-style dining or a full-service car wash versus a self-service one. In schools, common areas where the degree of involvement is part of the product decision include homework policies and the role of volunteerism in the school. In terms of volunteerism, it is wrong to

assume that it is merely a strategy to keep labor costs down. In fact, with many target markets of parents, volunteerism is an expectation. They *want* to be active in their children's education. In such a case, if the school does not understand the importance of working with volunteers effectively and respectfully, this can create problems with the school's relationship with its customers. If volunteerism is expected to be a key aspect of a school's product, it should be carefully managed using a volunteer coordinator who understands the importance of an effective volunteer program. The volunteer program should be treated as important and as an integral part of how the school operates, including integration throughout operations of the school (that is, not just the stuff that teachers and staff do not like to do). Schools with excellent volunteer programs do not just happen—they are created and managed by customers who truly want this as part of the school's product and by school leaders who embrace this with enthusiasm and relevance. The same analysis comes into play with homework. The leadership of the school must understand the parents' expectations in this area. How active do the parents want to be in the education of their children? How much does homework shape the perception of school quality?

3. *Intensity of service:* The level of awareness the customer has of the service and the delivery of that service is known as its *intensity.* For example, a less intensive business would be a yard-service company that may provide service when the customer is not even around. A more intense service would be haircutting, where the client is actively aware of the service as it happens. An entrepreneur can make some decisions about the degree of intensity with any business, but intensity is more often built into the very nature of the service and must be recognized realistically. In a school, communication with the parent is a good example of a factor over which the leadership has some degree of control over intensity. New electronic systems, which can integrate e-mail, voice mail, and the Internet into a single system, offer an incredible opportunity for an intensity of service with the parents. Systems exist that allow for automatic e-mail alerts to parents about upcoming assignments, student grades on past assignments, missed work, and

important dates. A website can create either synchronous (live chat rooms) or asynchronous (threaded discussion boards) discussion between the teacher and parents about classroom issues. Voice-mail alerts can be issued for more pressing issues or as follow-up. Technology can do almost anything that a school wants in the area of school information systems. However, two questions should guide the degree of its use and the complexity of the systems chosen. First, what can the school afford? These systems can become quite expensive in terms of initial cost as well as ongoing maintenance, licensing fees, and added technical staff. Second, what do the parents really want? The capacity of such systems to create unwanted information overload is not uncommon. Some target markets may not want the intensity of services that the school offers to them. Again, knowing the needs and wants of the customer is critical to getting this part of the product correct.

4. *Timing of services:* A variety of decisions arise regarding the timing of the services in a school. What will the school calendar be? If the school (for example, a new private high school) offers only certain grade levels, the leadership must decide whether it will create its own school calendar, follow that of the local public schools, or follow that of private elementary schools that feed it students. If not thought through carefully, the calendar can create havoc with family vacation planning if they have children in multiple school systems. Will the school follow the academic or a year-round schedule? The number of year-round schools, both public and private, continues to grow. There are various curricular, administrative, competitive, and financial considerations that guide such a decision. What will be the starting and ending times of the school? What services will be offered before and after the traditional school day? All these timing-of-services issues can become quite complex and are rarely easy decisions to make. Additionally, for many start-up schools, some or all of these may be out of the control of the school. A school may be using shared space. For example, the founders of one charter school found space in an old Catholic school that had closed. However, the building was still used by the parish for religious education on Wednesday nights and weekends. Additionally, the parish had

existing contracts to rent out some of the school space for evening events and summer camps. The charter school was forced to work around this schedule. This same school had to rely on public schools buses for transportation. The public school system had a policy that had charter schools last on the priority list for bus use. This meant that the school had to start much later in the day than it had originally planned. Ideally, the customer should at least in part be able to determine the timing of services. But this is not always going to be possible for start-up schools on tight budgets. The school should investigate this in advance so that realistic expectations can be established with their families.

PRICING

Pricing is the second part of the marketing mix. *Pricing* includes what is charged for the overall services offered by the school plus any additional fees or charges that may arise for its customers. For some schools, the pricing issue is moot, such as with charter schools that have their per pupil revenues determined by state statute. Other schools develop a simple model for pricing. For example, Mathew Metz, principal of St. Ambrose Catholic School in Woodbury, Minnesota, states that his school uses "a cost-based tuition system. Whatever it costs per child who walks through the door is what we charge for tuition." It should be noted that this method works only as long as enrollments are basically at capacity since the average cost will include both fixed costs (such as rent and salaries) and variable costs (such as food and supplies). This is discussed in more detail in chapter 9.

For many new schools today, pricing is not so simple. Decisions will need to be made on pricing, and these decisions will affect the financial health of the school. In education, as in almost any service business, parents look at value when they evaluate pricing. Value is the ratio of perceived quality over cost. Parents are willing to pay more for an education if they perceive that it is of superior quality. Although public school systems have an inherent price advantage (that is, public education is "free"), parents will choose to pay a higher price if they perceive the quality of private education to be significantly better, thus yielding a greater value. Pricing is both a science and an art. There are certain aspects of pricing that can be determined systematically; others require subjective decisions and even intuition.

The science part of pricing starts with an understanding of basic economics. Generally, and all things being equal, pricing is a function of supply and demand. If demand is low and supply is high, prices will be forced down. If demand is high and supply is low, prices will be forced up. Therefore, if there are a large number of high-quality educational choices in a community, this will push overall tuition levels down in that community. Conversely, where few good school choices exist, this will allow for higher levels of tuition to be charged.

The other part of the science of pricing depends good research. A thorough understanding of the pricing of all competitors helps one understand market pricing conditions. The structure of competitor's pricing (what is and is not included in tuition) also should be understood. Generally, customers will evaluate not only the base tuition but also all other fees and costs associated with each school. Part of pricing research can include asking a few potential customers what they would be willing to pay. It is important to understand that if given a choice among prices, most customers will tend to pick the lowest. Therefore, the wording should be carefully developed to get an accurate reading of how much customers would agreeably spend for the services provided. It often works best to pay for an independent survey that does not mention the new school by name. This will tend to result in more reliable data.

There also are subjective issues in pricing, as not all things are in fact equal, as the economic view would assume. A myth of many new entrepreneurs in any market is that they will have to charge much less than current prices in the market to attract new customers. This may or may not be true as customer perceptions come into play. If a school is able to define an image of superior quality, higher prices can be charged. If fact, simply having higher prices may create the perception in the minds of customers that a business is of higher quality. This is particularly true if quality is hard to assess. For example, a psychiatrist had planned to phase out of his private practice. He decided to raise his fees for any new patients by 50 percent. Rather than decreasing new business, it actually increased it. So he raised it again, so that his fees were now double what they had been. His practice then got even more new patients. The higher the price, the higher the customer perceived the quality of his services since the quality of psychiatric care is so hard to measure in any objective way. A similar example can be found in a university setting. A well-regarded liberal arts college charged a relatively high tuition. Some of its faculty would often moonlight at the local community college to earn extra money. When they did, they taught the same course with the same texts at both schools. Students who were transferring in from these community colleges often found that many courses would not transfer in, including the courses taught by the moonlighting faculty. Many of the students ended up taking the same course over, paying many times more than they did the first time at the community college. What was most surprising was how few families actually complained. Many just assumed that the course must somehow be better when it was taught at the liberal arts college.

PLACE

Thirty years ago, the term *place* in education would simply refer to the physical location of a school building. The options for place in education can now transcend the school building. Home schooling, Internet education, and experientially based internship programs are just some examples of new options for what can be considered a classroom.

However, for most schools the decision on a location is still extremely important. For a start-up school, there are three primary issues to consider when choosing a location. First, the location of a school building is still important in terms of the cost of the facility. Property values can vary widely within a single community. Second, convenience of the facility is important in that it will define in part the market for the school. Although some families will be willing to drive longer distances to attend a certain school, many will not. Thus, proximity to the areas where the primary target market lives becomes important. Proximity also will impact transportation costs if busing is provided. Third, general safety of the location will be a factor in many prospective customers' decision about the school.

Finding a location for a new school can be more difficult than it at first appears. Availability of space that is both large enough and adequate to house a school can be a challenge. If existing space is available it may not have enough larger rooms for classrooms or may not meet local or state standards for construction in schools. For example, a charter school was being developed to serve the Hispanic community in St. Paul, Minnesota. The largest concentration of Hispanic families resided in two general areas of the city. By far the largest concentration was in an area known as the "West Side." After putting together specifications for a building, the founding team set out to find possible sites to choose from in the West Side area. However, after several months of searching, not a single space could be found that would even marginally accommodate the new school. Eventually, the founders had to choose a site in the second area, which actually was several miles from the West Side. This had a significantly negative impact on the school's first-year enrollments because, although many West Side families wanted to enroll their children in the school, they did not want them to be bused out of their community.

Community issues may come into play for some possible locations. Although schools are generally thought to make great neighbors, it is more and more common for neighborhoods to fight new schools, particularly if they are not going to serve the children of the immediate neighborhood as the primary market. This can be even more of an issue if the school serves certain populations of students. For example, one alternative school for troubled teens had to spend months convincing a neighborhood that they could be a positive addition to their community. It took several community meetings and many hours of negotiation to finally gain support for the new school.

PROMOTION

As stated earlier in this chapter, advertising and promotion are what most people think of as marketing. Indeed, promotion is a key part of marketing but is only one part of an effective marketing plan.

The goal of *promotion* is finding effective means to communicate with customers and potential customers about the product. The key is to understand the process that customers follow when making decisions about which school is right for their children. Where do they seek out information to make this decision? What type of information do they want? What form is best for providing this information? How do they make their decision on which school they will choose once they have this information?

As discussed in chapter 5, competitive analysis and market research provide a clear picture of what is important to parents in their school choice. Schools should use what they have learned from this information and find effective methods to communicate what will make their school better. An old marketing adage is "Think like your customer." The school must learn how parents gather information to make their decisions and make sure the information the school wants to communicate is effectively delivered within that context. A good example can be seen in higher education. Over the past few years, parents and high school students have begun to rely more and more on the Internet to gather information about colleges. Colleges that have recognized this trend and have found effective ways to get their "message out" through this new medium often have a distinct competitive advantage.

Start-ups find that advertising and promotion can be expensive if not properly managed. Many find the principles of bootstrap marketing to be highly beneficial. Bootstrapping refers to any process that helps a business accomplish its goals and objectives with limited resources and comes from the old phrase "pulling oneself up by one's bootstraps." The goal of bootstrap marketing is to get as much attention as possible for the school with its customers when faced with the reality of minimal cash for such activities.

There are five basic principles of bootstrap marketing:

1. *Use only media that the customer will use in decision making to communicate with the customer:* If, for example, most customers use phone book ads to find your particular type of business, then you should use such ads. But if customers never look for your type of business in phone book ads, then advertising there is a waste of your precious cash flow. Again, think like the customer.
2. *Focus is on the impact of message, not just its volume:* Expensive media blitzes are not always the key to success in promot-

ing the business. Getting messages to customers in a way that influences their decisions and that will be remembered is the objective.

3. *Focus on the benefit that the service will bring to the customer:* Make a clear statement of what makes the school unique. Why should customers choose this school over others?

4. *Understand the market niche that the school occupies and how to position the school within that niche:* A school within a specific niche may promote in a completely different manner than a similar business with a much broader market. For example, a national fast-food franchise promotes in a very different manner than does a local neighborhood restaurant. Each should have completely different promotional plans.

5. *Keep it simple and cheap:* Most entrepreneurs must use bootstrap marketing early in the business's development to preserve cash flow. But the message must still get out in order to attract needed customers.

Ramona Rosales, executive director of Academia Cesar Chavez, describes her school's use of bootstrap promotion during its start-up:

> Our first problem was in the recruitment of students. There tends to be somewhat of a negative image of charter schools because a couple in the state have had problems. We had to gain the trust of the parents in the community before our school could really succeed. This year being year 2, we have most classes with waiting lists, and we only had to recruit fifty students for next year, so I feel we have been able to gain the trust of parents needed for our school.

To promote the new charter school, the leadership team went to community day events, parades, churches, and other community events in their target neighborhoods to provide potential customers with information about the school. The most effective medium to communicate the message was face-to-face contact. Parents wanted to meet those running the new school and get their specific questions answered. The impact of this message was immediate, as many families signed up at each event. The message was not wasted through a broad promotion that would have reached uninterested people outside their target market. The cost was minimal for this campaign. They printed simple yet clear brochures. They handed out application packets to those who seemed interested. Other than that, the only other cost was their time.

The notion that marketing is a process and not an event holds true for promotion. It is important to continually bring the message to its intended audiences. Schools should avoid the roller-coaster ride of only promoting when enrollments get a little soft. By then, the impact on revenues is already being felt in the school, and the time to create any impact from the "crisis" promotional campaign may be too long. Marketing and promotion should be a consistent part of business operations.

A school should understand that it has multiple levels of customers. Clearly, the parents are the primary decision makers. However, the children also will be a part of the decision in many families. Part of the promotional plan should address them as well. If outside funding and support comes to the school (such as state funding for charter schools or parish support for parochial schools), then part of the promotional plan should address these constituencies as well.

There are a variety of tools and techniques that a school can use for promotion. Not every school should even consider all of these. Again, it will be helpful to understand how the intended customers make their decisions and how information can be best provided to shape those decisions in the school's direction. A promotional budget should be carefully developed and make sense within the overall available budget. Even modest promotional budgets can be effective. Once the budget is established, it should be followed. Impulsive decisions for new promotional ideas can quickly bust the limited budget of any school.

The following summarizes a variety of promotional tools that a school may want to consider utilizing:

PUBLICITY

- Publicity is free advertising.
- The most effective method of obtaining publicity in local media is through the use of press releases. When preparing a press release,

there are methods to get the attention of those who would use the material in their newspaper, magazine, or radio or television program. Anticipate the story angle that will convince the media to use the story. The quality of writing is extremely important. It helps to include a cover letter or relevant article to clarify the story. Following up with a phone call to "sell" the story also can be advantageous.

BUSINESS CARDS

- The business card often is the first form of promotion that a potential customer may see from a business, and yet many times little attention is paid to its design.
- Just a small increase in spending on business cards can have a significant impact on their effectiveness. A cheap-looking and even cheap-feeling card communicates that the business is not professional and reflects the quality of the business itself. The quality of the paper is critical to an effective card.
- A well-designed card includes all critical information and leaves out insignificant data.

BROCHURES

- Brochures provide a visual presentation of what might be communicated in a face-to-face contact.
- If well designed and written, brochures can increase the credibility of a start-up school.
- Design issues are important for an effective brochure. Paper quality and the use of color should match the message and desired image the school is promoting. Simplicity is sometimes best, depending on the customer's expectations. An overly produced brochure can communicate wasteful spending as quickly as a poorly designed one can suggest incompetence.
- The brochure should include a clear headline, be visually appealing, be easy to read, tell the school's "story" and mission, include testimonials, and include useful contact information.

NEWSLETTERS

- Newsletters can be an effective means of communication for both current and potential customers. To ensure they are read, newsletters should be interesting, informative, and educational.
- All written materials should be carefully proofread before printing. Multiple typos do not reflect well on the school.
- Highlight students, family, teachers, and staff.
- Keep consistent in terms of its look, feel, theme, and focus.
- Once the newsletter begins publication, make sure to have the staff and resources to continue its production.

WEBSITES

- Make sure customers will use the website to make decisions. It is a myth that all businesses must have a website to be successful.
- Appearing on search engines can be key if the website is being used to attract new customers.
- Websites may be useful as tool only for existing customers. Make sure to think like the customers and understand if and how they would use a web page.
- Budget for maintenance. Keeping the website up-to-date takes time and money, and outdated web pages do not reflect well on the organization.

PHONE BOOK ADS

- Advertising in phone books can be quite expensive, so it is important to plan carefully and consider whether the intended customers will actually use such ads. This may not be a wise use of scarce dollars for many schools. Each entry into the different categories of the phone book ad section will cost additional money, so choosing the one best entry is critical. A school should avoid entering multiple ads in different entries.
- If phone book ads are used, the format does matter. Customers will judge legitimacy to some degree by the relative size of the ad when compared to the other competitors in the same section.

- Color can help if there are many entries under a heading. Illustrations or logos also can make the ad stand out.
- Within the copy, stress integrity and the scope of services offered and offer easy directions to the facility.

NEWSPAPER ADS

- Newspaper ads are most effective if they use any of a variety of techniques to draw the reader's attention, including a strong headline, pictures, a border, and/or color.
- Include plenty of written information. After all, it is a newspaper, and people are expecting to read. This information can include testimonials, offers to get customers to act, and easy contact information, including phone numbers, address, e-mail, and web address.
- Placement within the newspaper does matter. Again, think like the intended customer and put the ad where it is most likely to be seen by your target market. For example, because men are the primary purchasers of car tires, most ads for tire stores are found in the sports section of the paper.

VIDEO BROCHURES

- Videos can be a powerful medium to tell a school's story.
- High-quality production is important, but this can come at a high price. Most videos can cost $1,000 to $5,000 per minute of final video run time.
- A five-minute video should be adequate. Potential customers may not watch anything longer than that.
- Each copy can cost as much as $10 to copy and mail to prospective customers, so care should be taken to send videos only to truly interested families.

MAGAZINE ADS

- Although magazines can be expensive, they work well if properly targeted and if the market is from a broad enough region (for example,

residential schools). Size, color, and photographs get more attention. Ads with pictures of people tend to draw attention as well.
- Position does not matter, except on covers.

RADIO

- More private schools are beginning to use radio advertising. For example, a conservative Catholic prep school found it highly effective to advertise on local conservative talk format radio stations. Radio is a highly targeted medium, and for this school it was a cost-effective means to reach the target market. In addition, the most cost-effective way to use this medium is to use only one or two stations that best fit the target market for the school.
- Radio is generally used to reinforce other promotional media, such as newspaper ads and websites.

TELEVISION

- With the proliferation of cable television stations, some schools have found this to be an effective medium. In fact, ads shown on cable can run for as little as $100 per spot.
- Television ads work best if they are clear, visual, and use good-quality production.

In summary, the following are important aspects of an effective promotional plan:

- Clearly identify all the benefits the product or service offers to the customers, particularly those that are unique.
- Clearly identify the market niche of the business and the specific characteristics of the niche and its customers.
- Clearly identify the target customers and target market.
- Develop the key promotion strategies and the positioning of the product or service in the market.
- Establish an affordable promotional budget that can have the needed impact.

- Identify the specific promotional tools and techniques.
- Develop a clear month-by-month timetable.
- Monitor and review the progress of meeting the timetable.

CUSTOMER RELATIONS

Rather than only focusing on attracting new customers, a business also must pay attention to keeping the customers it already has. This is known as *customer relations*. Managing customer relations in a smaller organization, like the typical school, is best understood in terms of managing the relationship through day-to-day interactions. What are the various ways that the customer comes in contact with the school? What do they experience each time they come in contact with the school? Can improvements be made in each type of contact they have with all parts of the school? It is critical to look at the school as the customer does and understand what their day-to-day interactions with the business may be like.

Several examples can illustrate how this is done. One owner of a fast-food restaurant would ask her friends to go through the drive-through as ordinary customers and describe what the experience was like. They reported on timeliness, friendliness, and accuracy. Shift teams that earned high marks were rewarded with bonuses. Most real estate agents suggest that a family selling a home begin entering through the front door when preparing to sell their home to see it as prospective buyers will. One business owner was concerned about the new automated phone and voice-mail system he had just installed. One month after its installation, he called his best customers to see whether they liked the system. Although they liked the voice-mail system, they hated the automated answering system, some even saying they were less likely to call the business because of it. Within a week, the business owner hired a receptionist.

For most businesses, it is many times less expensive to keep a customer than it is to attract a new one, yet customer relations are not emphasized enough by many businesses. Marketing mix, product, pricing, place, and promotion should be created with an eye toward keeping existing customers, not just toward attracting new ones. An old adage in sales is that it is just as important to "close the back door to keep a customer with you as it is to open the front door to let them in."

SUMMARY

This chapter examined each of the four parts of the marketing plan—product, pricing, promotion, and place—in detail. Once the most effective strategy for focusing on these four parts of marketing is developed, the entrepreneur should create a marketing plan and budget to guide marketing activities for the new school. The marketing plan should include a well-developed promotional plan that integrates all the promotional efforts that the school intends to use in attracting customers. The promotional plan should identify the message that needs to be communicated, the media that best deliver that message to parents, and a clear budget to implement that plan. Effective management of the day-to-day relationship between the school and its customers also is an important part of marketing. The next chapter moves away from markets and marketing and examines the process of creating the right team to lead the new school.

CHAPTER 7

The Team

Success in start-up organizations depends on entrepreneurs recognizing that they cannot succeed by acting alone. Part of the planning process, even before a new business starts, is to evaluate the expertise, talents, and knowledge that the new entity will require from its leadership. The leadership team for a school includes not only the management team who operates the school on a day-to-day basis but also its board. (The term *board* is used to represent the legal governing body of the school. Depending on the type of school entity and legal form of organization the school takes, it could be formally known as a board of directors, board of trustees, school board, and so forth.) In addition, the team can and should include people beyond the board and the management staff, including outside advisers and consultants. The founders must ensure that all necessary talent and expertise is available as the school grows and develops, wherever it may come from. This chapter examines the process of needs assessment, planning, and developing the team to support a new school during its planning, start-up, and growth.

THE TEAM DURING THE PRELAUNCH PHASE

Even during the prelaunch phase of developing a school (when the vision is defined and the basic feasibility is assessed), the formation of the school's leadership team is beginning to take place. Most founding teams include some combination of educators or parents, that is, like-minded people coming together around a common purpose. This is true in any business start-up. In fact, one of the problems seen in many start-ups is that the founders have *too much* in common. They may be classmates from a university who have shared a common course of study. They may be coworkers who come from the same department in the business in which they all work. They may simply be friends who come together to pursue a common dream for independence. In the case of a proposed new school, they may be a group of parents wishing to create a school with a different culture or specialized focus, or they may be a group of teachers who want to serve a particular population of students.

Time and time again, those who work with start-ups of all types see two critical problems that can arise from such "leadership inbreeding." First, the team may be concentrated around a single set of skills. For example, all the founders may be educators. Such a team may lack the financial and managerial skills necessary to succeed in a new school start-up. A residential school start-up that was founded by child therapists experienced this problem. Not only did they lack the financial and managerial skills, they even lacked basic classroom management and curriculum skills. Second, leadership inbreeding can lead to a myopic approach to making decisions. If the leadership shares common experiences and backgrounds, they may lack the diversity of thought that can help support creative problem solving.

Board

A formal board is required by law for most types of schools organizations. The board is a key part of the team for a new school well before the school doors actually open for students. The functions and responsibilities of such a board mirrors those of a traditional public school board. The board will have the ultimate accountability for both the management and the financial oversight of the school it oversees. However, since most school start-ups are organized through legal incorporation, there are additional roles and responsibilities for their boards.

A traditional public school board is directly accountable to the community, as voters in the community almost always elect its members. It also will have a direct relationship with government entities that provide funding at the local, county, and state levels. Start-up schools are often established as nonprofit or for-profit corporations. As such, there is a discrete set of issues that the board will need to address as a corporation. Their relationships to the various stakeholders can be quite different, and these differences range from subtle to fundamental. For example, the relationship of a public school board to its parents is such that if they are not satisfied with the performance of the board, the parents and other citizens can vote the board out of office. In a private school, charter school, and so forth, the relationship to the parents is clearly more of a customer relationship. In many cases, parents' ultimate displeasure can be voiced only by withdrawing their children from the school.

During the prelaunch phase, the board may not be formally active beyond any legal requirements needed to establish the corporation that is used to organize the school. As the school develops, the board has legal authority and responsibility over several specific areas. Subsequent sections of this chapter examine these responsibilities as they become pertinent for the board as the school develops.

For some schools, key leaders will have multiple roles. That is, the school's board may include members who also hold management roles. In a for-profit school, some or all of the board members also may be shareholders of the corporation. There are very specific *legal* differences between the actions of these individuals in their roles as owners, board members, and officers in a corporation. In a for-profit school entity, the shareholders or owners have very limited responsibilities and should take great care not to stray beyond these roles. One of the main reasons to become incorporated is to create a legal barrier between any legal liability of the owners as shareholders and as individuals. For example, assume that a school faces a lawsuit for an injury that occurred on the school grounds. The corporation would face any financial liability that may arise from this incident, while the owners, as individuals, would be protected by law from this liability. This is known as the *corporate veil of protection.* However, if the owners of this corporation stray beyond the specific responsibilities they have under the law, they can create a situation in which they expose themselves to liability *as individuals.*

Several individuals decided to create a residential school for emotionally and behaviorally disturbed teenage boys. Most of the founders also invested in the corporation by becoming shareholders. As the school developed, the founding group took on roles that fit their skills, education, and experience. That meant that some of the owners of the business assumed roles that were not a part of the management group. Some were teachers, and some were counselors. One teacher took great delight in pointing out that she was not only a teacher but an owner as well. She would use this as a means to "get what she wanted" and to "tell other staff what to do." In addition to being bad for morale, this behavior ran the risk of sliding into a situation where she was making an operational decision with no other authority than that which she had as an owner. That is, her job in the school did not give her the authority to act as she did. In fact, she ran some risk of creating personal liability for herself *as a shareholder* in the corporation that would not be protected by the corporate veil of liability protection. Fortunately, the corporate attorney for the school provided training to the board that delineated the legal roles and responsibilities of the owners, the board, and the management. With this knowledge, the teacher was confronted about the possible legal implications of her actions, and she changed her behaviors in the school.

Shareholders in a corporation have the following responsibilities:

Elect board members
Vote on dividends
Amend bylaws and other corporate documents
Approve sale of the business

Beyond these actions, shareholders in a corporation delegate all other responsibilities to the board and/or management. For many corporations, the shareholders meet only once a year. Beyond informational items, the actual business portion of the meeting is generally brief.

Similar situations also have been observed in charter schools, where teachers are required (in some states) to serve on the board. Care must be taken to train these teachers as to their specific legal roles and responsibilities. They need to understand that in the day-to-day operation of the school, their actions should be guided by their job descriptions and not at all influenced by their separate role as board members. They should act only as board members in formal board meetings.

The Management Team

During the prelaunch phase, the management team is engaged primarily in the process of creating the vision and assessing the feasibility of the new school (see chapters 2 and 3). Specific roles in the development of the vision and in the feasibility analysis of the school should be taken on the basis of the experience, education, and skills of the various team members. The temptation may be to run everything as a committee of equals. This can work during the prelaunch phase, but it should be clearly understood by all that this is only temporary. As the school moves toward opening, clearly defined roles and reporting relationships must be established and followed. Certainly the school can develop a culture that supports a participatory style of management, but at some point clear lines of authority and accountability will need to be put in place. To avoid any misunderstandings later on, it is critical to have open and honest discussions on all of this very early in the development of the school. It is never too early to address these issues. If approached objectively—on the basis of experience, educational training, and skills—these issues can usually be resolved fairly easily. If not, outside board members and advisers can serve as mediators.

In the prelaunch phase, the team should include, at a minimum, individuals with expertise in curriculum, administration, and financial management. As the school moves closer to opening, these areas of expertise may evolve into specific jobs. For example, the founder with expertise in financial management may become the business manager of the school, while the founder with more curriculum expertise may become the person responsible for supervision of all classroom activities. In a small start-up school with limited budgets, it is important for everyone to understand that they may have to take on multiple roles.

Advisers and Consultants

Dedicated advisers are an invaluable resource for a start-up school. It is not at all uncommon to be able to recruit highly skilled individuals to serve as advisers at no cost to the school. These people often simply have a strong personal interest in promoting certain types of schools, be they parochial, charter, and so forth. Such volunteers may be willing to

put in dozens of pro bono hours helping in financial planning, legal issues, curriculum development, building planning and construction, and
general management consulting. Many of these individuals also may be
willing to serve on the formal board as the school moves ahead.

THE TEAM DURING THE PLANNING PHASE

To avoid the potentially fatal problems that can arise from leadership
inbreeding discussed earlier in this chapter, part of the process of the
business planning should include a careful assessment of the leadership
team. Table 7.1 displays a format that can be used for this assessment.

Table 7.1.   Entrepreneurial Self-Assessment

Skills	Strong	Adequate	Weak
Financial and technology management			
Budgeting and cash flow management			
Technology assessment and planning			
Credit and collections			
Banking relationships, grant writing, and other forms of raising funds			
Financial modeling			
Accounting/control			
General managerial			
Planning and goal setting			
Purchasing			
Team building			
Persuasion and negotiating			
Organizing			
Developing and managing human resources (recruiting/hiring, training/ development, salary, benefits, disciplining, etc.)			
Curriculum development and assessment			
Classroom and facility planning			
Leadership			
Delegating authority and responsibility			
Communicating values, beliefs, and norms			
Ability to seek advice/counsel			
Ability to formulate and communicate vision			
Mind-set			
Flexibility/adaptability			
Self-reliance			
Persistence			
Ability to focus on essentials			
Goal direction			

Note. Adapted from Cornwall and Carter (2000).

The team assessment should begin with a thorough evaluation of the skills and experiences of each member of the founding team. The results of the individual assessments should then be aggregated to show any potential gaps in the team's expertise and experience that will need to be filled as the school develops. Additional staff members, board members, advisers, or consultants may fill these gaps. Although the assessment should include educational competence in curriculum and classroom issues, it also needs to address a much broader array of managerial skills. The assessment also should evaluate financial, managerial, human resource, leadership, and technology skills.

Financial management is a major part of the success or failure of most school start-ups. For example, financial distress is the biggest cause of most charter school failures. Good financial management requires two basic sets of skills: knowing what funding is needed and managing the available funding. Any start-up school should make sure to have a member on the management team who has good financial skills. Specifically, the following areas of expertise are essential:

- *Financial modeling* is the process of forecasting the uses and sources of funding for a start-up school. It is a different process than many experienced school administrators have come across during the time they may have spent in public schools or even established private schools. As is discussed in chapter 9, it is a process that requires extrapolating revenues and expenses from market research and other analyses performed in feasibility analysis and business planning.
- *Budgeting* is the process of taking data from past experience (with the exception of the first year of operation) and planning data for the next year to develop specific targets for revenue and spending.
- *Cash flow management* is the process of managing the actual cash available on a day-to-day, week-to-week, and month-to-month basis. Effective cash flow management entails managing not only the expenditure of funds but also credit and collections from tuition, public funding, and grants.
- Another key part of financial management includes effectively *managing banking relationships*. This is discussed in detail later in this chapter.

- Most start-up schools will need to seek funding from a variety of sources, so expertise in *grant writing and other forms of raising funds* is an important skill to have on the team.
- Once the school is operational, sound *accounting and financial control* systems will need to be developed to provide the types of financial reporting that both the management team and external funders will demand.
- Adequately managing the financial demands of any organization requires at least a basic *ability to manage information technology systems.* Most schools can get all the information they need from fairly simple accounting and spreadsheet systems that are available for purchase "off the shelf."

General management expertise includes several varied skills:

- From the very beginning of the period before the start-up of the school, *planning and goal setting* should be a regular part of the management team's activities. The planning discipline that is developed before the school opens should become part of the general routine as the school continues to grow.
- *Purchasing systems* will need to be put in place to ensure that the budget maintains its integrity over the course of the year. External funding sources and the Internal Revenue Service will insist that adequate controls be developed for the purchasing process.
- As new staff members are hired, management must be able to continue to build the team spirit that the founding group developed before the opening of the school. This is a process that must be actively managed. *Teams and teamwork* do not develop without active and conscious management by the leadership group.
- *Persuasion and negotiation* are critical management skills that will come into play in working with potential sources of funding. They also are important skills on the expenditure side as major contracts, such as the lease for the building, food service, transportation, phone service, and so forth, are secured.
- As the staff grows, the ability to effectively *organize and manage the human resources* of the school will grow more complex. Fi-

nally, management must have the necessary expertise in curriculum, classroom, and facility planning for a growing school.

Leadership skills are often overlooked in start-up schools. Leadership is much more than just being able to persuade others to do what you need them to do (leadership is discussed in more detail in chapter 11):

- Leadership also includes the ability to effectively *delegate responsibility and authority.* It is important to note that leaders most likely are better at delegating the former than the latter.
- Leaders must be diligent about *communicating the culture* of the school (values, norms, and beliefs). Culture must be consciously managed, especially as the school grows and staff turnover occurs over time.
- Effective leaders must have the ability to *seek advice and council* when needed. No one can be expected to know everything about every issue.
- Leaders must have the ability to *formulate and communicate the vision* for the new school to new staff and to outside stakeholders.

There also is an entrepreneurial mind-set that has proven to be important for start-up endeavors. Not all team members need to have all or even part of this entrepreneurial mind-set, but it is advantageous to have the following four characteristics of this way of thinking represented among the entrepreneurial team:

- *Flexibility and adaptability* to changing circumstances can prove to be essential. As was discussed earlier in this book, most opportunities for new schools are a result of some sort of change. However, by its very nature, change is not static. Therefore, the same ability to recognize the sources of opportunity should be applied as the school grows. Change is continuous, and the school must continuously adapt to change.
- Successful entrepreneurs must often be *self-reliant.* The experience of being an entrepreneur has often been described as a lonely one. Although the entrepreneur develops a team to support his or

her efforts, ultimately some decisions and challenges must rest with the entrepreneur.

- To be successful, entrepreneurs must be *persistent*. This requires patience, as achieving progress often can take much time and effort.
- The *ability to focus* on the fundamental goals and issues that will help achieve success is an essential part of the entrepreneurial mind-set. Distractions can arise from many directions. New opportunities, nonessential problems, other peoples' personal priorities, and so forth may take the entrepreneur's focus away from the essential. The entrepreneur must be able to identify what is truly important and then block the rest out. The business plan can prove to be an important tool to support this type of single-minded focus.

Once the assessment of the founding team is complete, the next step is to create a leadership plan. The first step in developing this plan is to create an inventory of anticipated leadership skills and attributes. Knowledge and experience in the various areas listed previously can vary widely. A school will not necessarily need a highly educated and trained corporate chief financial officer type to handle the financial management of the school. Therefore, the following questions need to be asked in each skill area:

What will be the levels of expertise required in each of the critical skills that the school will require from its team?

What will be the scope of each skill required? Can a part-time staff person manage it? Can a volunteer adviser provide enough time and expertise to cover certain needs? Are consultants the most effective method?

Since not all the needs will have to be addressed at once, a plan should be created that includes the anticipated timing of each need. Some systems will need to be in place when the school opens its doors. Others can evolve as the school grows. Still others may not be required until the school is near its capacity. The financial realities of the school also dictate timing. Many schools simply cannot afford certain types of highly paid employees, especially in the early stages when cash flow is very limited. The school leadership may simply need to "make do" and get by as best they can until funding can support certain staff. For example, one charter school determined that it needed a reasonably experienced financial manager because of the complexity and variety of its funding sources. The information they required in funding applications and in the follow-up reports was fairly complex. Although a full-time person would have been ideal, the budget simply did not allow for this person until the second year of operation. Instead, one member of the leadership team worked with an outside adviser to get by in this area for the first year. Although not an ideal situation, the arrangement worked until the budget allowed for the addition of a full-time person with this expertise in the second year. Therefore, the team plan should identify where the various needs can realistically be filled: management, the board, volunteer advisers, or paid consultants. This should be part of the business plan and should include a clear outline of priorities and time lines.

The Role of the Board during the Planning Phase

Even before the school becomes operational, the board has a variety of responsibilities:

- The board is responsible for *selecting the top manager of the school.* The title of this position can vary widely: principal, director, or headmaster. In a for-profit school, this person will likely carry a legally required title of president of the corporation. Once selected, the board also is required to evaluate and, if necessary, terminate the top school manager.
- Often, the board will *approve senior management* for the start-up of the school. Although the top management will conduct the search and make recommendations, usually the initial team is approved by the board. Once operational, this becomes the duty of the top manager.
- The board *nominates other board members.* Although some board members may think differently, the term of members on the board is not a life sentence. Typically, board members will serve two- or three-year terms that may or may not be renewable for a certain

number of additional terms (it is advisable to have some limit on the number of terms). The board is responsible to help recruit and approve new members. Some boards also may decide to expand membership to bring in more expertise or to attract potential funders. For example, a therapeutic preschool deliberately grew a fairly large board made up mainly of wealthy business leaders who had a personal interest in the school. Those board members all became major benefactors of the school as well.

- During planning, the board will begin the process of *approving major policies* that will guide the administration of the school.

The leadership of the school, particularly the top manager, should learn how to both use and manage the board effectively. Those with experience working with volunteer boards have found the following to enhance the effectiveness of these boards:

- *Work with each board member as an individual:* Make sure to understand the expertise that each member can offer and to know the issues that will be most important to each. Some members will be most concerned with curriculum issues, some with financial management, and some with risk management.
- *Be honest and forthright with the board:* Establish the board's trust, and never attempt to keep critical information from them. They have a right and a duty to know what is going on in the school. They do not need to know the day-to-day managerial issues, but they do need to know about major events, be they good or bad.
- *Establish clear expectations on the roles and responsibilities of the board from the start:* This includes such simple but critical issues as attendance at meetings.
- *Make clear the role, scope of authority, and expected behavior of the board:* The management team should, in turn, make clear their responsibility to the board.

Someone must take the responsibility to manage the board meetings and agendas in a deliberate manner. If the top manager of the school does not fill this role directly (and they often cannot or should not because of conflicts of interest), then that manager should work very closely with the chair of the board to make sure that meetings go smoothly and that key actions and decisions get made on a timely basis. This requires communicating in advance about the topics for each meeting and getting any key materials to the board in advance.

The Role of Advisers and Consultants during the Planning Phase

In addition to any specialized consultants or advisers a school may use, there are three basic external consultants/advisers that every start-up business should have in place before it begins operations: a banker, an attorney, and an outside accountant.

Even though a school may not have the scope of funding needs that other start-up businesses require, there are many ways in which a good relationship with a banker is critical. Bankers can provide important management advice, as most work with dozens of entrepreneurial ventures at any given time and can see problems that they all share, particularly in the area of financial management. Schools often need the financial support that a bank can provide, such as short-term lines of credit or even financing for facilities and equipment. Therefore, understanding how banks make business loans and how to establish and nurture a good relationship with a banker should be part of the educational entrepreneur's financing plans.

A common assumption is that bankers lend on the basis of collateral. That is, if a school has assets to pledge, such as desks and computers, the banker will lend money without any question. In fact, banks make lending decisions on the basis of a much more complex set of criteria. The ability of the school to generate enough cash flow each month to easily make payments of interest and principal is the primary factor that any bank will use to determine whether it is willing to make a loan. Because most start-ups do not have much cash to speak of (to say nothing about excess cash each month), many banks are not willing to lend money to a true start-up school.

With a for-profit school, another criterion a banker will evaluate is the entrepreneur's ability to personally pay back the loan if the business fails. In some businesses, the bank may eventually lift this requirement, but only after the business reaches a point where the positive cash flow is so substantial that the business no longer carries significant risk, which is not common even among for-profit schools. The banker will ask for personal financial statements from all shareholders in the business. This will include a personal balance sheet, which shows personal assets and liabilities, and a personal income statement or tax return. The bank will focus primarily on what it considers personal liquid assets, such as cash and marketable securities, and free cash flow from each shareholder of the school. The bank asks for this information because it will almost always require that the entrepreneurs and their spouses personally guarantee the business loans as well. Even if the school enters bankruptcy and closes its doors, the banks want the ability to pursue repayment from the guarantors. In the case of a nonprofit school, the bank will not have the ability to seek personal guarantees since there are no real owners of the business.

Yet another criterion regards assets that serve as collateral to back the loan. Bankers have no interest in taking over a distressed school and even less interest in selling assets they can seize to pay off defaulted loans. Even if a school has valuable assets, such as a building and land that are owned without any encumbrance of debt, most banks will not lend money unless the school is generating strong cash flow.

Since most school start-ups are nonprofits and have little or no cash flow or valuable assets, does that mean that banks will not lend them money? The answer is no. Many banks have, as part of their mission, a commitment to support a certain number of community organizations. Does this mean that a school is entitled to bank support? Absolutely not. The bank still expects to get repaid. However, it may be willing to take *slightly* more risk on the school. At a minimum, the school will still need to demonstrate through its business plan that they can meet the payment obligations created by any loans. The better the business plan supports the fact that the school will actually have the cash flow the plan predicts, the more likely banks may issue loans to that school. The bank will also require that any assets that the school owns be pledged to the loan.

Even if the primary criteria are met, the bank will evaluate secondary criteria as well before committing to a loan. In fact, these secondary factors may become more important for a nonprofit school than for more traditional entrepreneurial businesses. Secondary factors that can be considered include the reputation, experience, and character of the founders and their board and the management capability available to the school through its team. The specific types of loans that schools may seek are discussed in chapter 9.

It is important to keep in mind that the relationship with a bank does not entail only the activities involved in securing the loan. Before a bank makes a loan to a school, certain information will need to be shared. And after a bank makes a loan, the relationship with the banker must be managed properly to ensure a good long-term relationship. There are three phases of the relationship with a bank:

1. *Initial contact with bankers:* First impressions *do* count when making contact with a banker. The school leaders should be fully prepared to provide a business plan and financial projections even at the initial meeting with the banker. The banker will be evaluating the management team's own understanding of the financial data and the assumptions used in generating projected financial statements.

   Banks will sometimes have a history of working with schools in the community. If they had favorable experiences with other schools, their perception reduces the credit risk of the next school that comes to them for financial support. Conversely, if the bank is relatively unfamiliar with lending to schools, this may increase their perception of credit risk. Information and experience reduces uncertainty for banks. Therefore, it is advisable for school founders to research which banks currently lend money to other schools. The chances of a favorable response will be much higher.

2. *Preparation of key loan documents:* These documents are the following:
   * *Loan proposal:* The first document generated by the bank is often a loan proposal. The loan proposal, also called a letter of commitment, outlines the general terms and conditions of the loan. This is the time when the school founder can try to negotiate certain items in the proposal. The loan proposal will include a variety of terms and conditions, including loan amount and interest rate, purpose of the loan, payment schedule, fees, collateral, conditions to be met before loan closing, restrictions

and reporting expectations, and events that are considered a default of the loan.

- *Loan document:* Once the loan proposal is agreed to and signed by both parties and fully executed, the bank will create the loan document, which is the legal documentation of the loan. This document will contain all the general terms, conditions, restrictions, and performance requirements agreed to in the loan proposal. The loan document may also contain additional terms and conditions that the school leader should carefully evaluate. Since getting a loan is a new experience for many school founders, this is an important time to utilize board members and advisers with business-loan experience to evaluate and explain the loan document. Although there is a real hesitancy to change the standard format of a loan document, there can be negotiation at this point as well, even on the standard contract language on the back of any standard form the bank uses. Every aspect of the loan document should be carefully considered, as it may have a significant impact on the operation of the school's going forward. For example, a loan agreement may include a clause in its standard agreement that prohibits a company from buying any assets over $50,000 without written permission of the bank. Given the cost of most office equipment and vehicles, this restriction could become a significant constraint to doing everyday business.

3. *Ongoing communication after the loan is made:* An old adage says "Bankers hate surprises." Loans are made to any entrepreneurial venture on the basis of anticipated future performance, which is reflected in its projected financial statements. The team will create projected financial statements by generating any number of assumptions regarding both revenues and expenses. It is the entrepreneur's responsibility to provide information to the banker on progress toward the projected financial performance. Banks will require certain financial statements at predetermined intervals of time, such as monthly, quarterly, or annually. To assist the banker in understanding the financial statements, the school leader also should provide updates on the key assumptions behind the projected financial statements so that any variances

from the projected financial forecasts and budgets can be understood. If assumptions prove to be significantly wrong or certain factors require assumptions to be changed, the school should inform the bank about the changing conditions, their impact on the school's future operations, and any steps the management team is taking to adjust for changing conditions as soon as possible.

For example, one charter school had modeled its financial projections assuming that the state funding would be remain on the same per pupil basis used for the past four years. However, after an election, the political climate changed, and the per pupil rate to charter schools dropped. The school's leadership revised their budget on the basis of the change and took measures to reduce expenses to cover the shortfall. They then immediately communicated the funding change and the steps they were taking to keep their budget in balance to their banker. Although the banker watched them somewhat more closely for a period of time to make sure that all of the adjusted plans were put into place, he remained confident that this school would stay a viable customer for the bank.

Regular communication with the banker can take both written and verbal forms. Some bankers would rather receive periodic formal written reports, which can be either print or electronic. Other banks may require only verbal updates, most often via regular telephone conversations. The type of communication requested by the bank typically is a function of the perceived risk of the loans. Therefore, if a bank had been satisfied with periodic phone calls in the past but now demands written updates, this likely is a signal that the bank has a increased concern with the performance of the school.

An attorney and an external accountant with experience in working with schools are the other two key advisers. The following can serve as a guide to hiring an attorney and an accountant:

- Get referrals from other school leaders, advisers, and board members and choose two or three to interview.
- Evaluate their personality and fit—whether they are good listeners and easy to talk to and whether they understand the needs of the school and are trustworthy.

- Evaluate their compatibility with the school's team.
- Determine their understanding of education organizations, particularly of the same type as the new start-up, such as charter school or religious school.
- Gain a clear understanding of billing policies (usually negotiable) and sensitivity to the school's budget constraints. For example, some firms may be willing to designate one of their staff to serve on the board without charge.

When working with accountants, attorneys, and any paid outside consultants, there are some steps that can be taken to ensure that costs be kept to a minimum while still getting the services the school needs. Outside consultants may be used to assist in areas such as curriculum design, space planning, grant writing, and technology planning:

- Prepare for meetings in advance and batch issues together. Do not bring in or call with only a single issue without making sure there are not other issues that could be discussed in the same conversation. This will lead to a more efficient use of their time and reduce their billable hours.
- Insist on the staff doing tasks that are routine. This can include typing documents, doing research, and even making photocopies.
- Keep in mind that there can be nontime charges that can amount to a surprisingly high bill, including travel, long-distance phone calls, faxing, and word processing.
- Keep them "up to speed" on progress toward goals and on any significant changes in the business plan.
- Discuss billing concerns openly.
- Always give them permission to challenge decisions and assumptions.

THE TEAM DURING THE START-UP AND OPERATING PHASE

Once the school is up and operating, the team's role continues to evolve. In addition to the responsibilities assumed during the phases before the start-up of the school, the board takes on the following:

- Approves the annual budget.
- Approves any new liabilities for the school (loans or larger long-term leases).
- Approves major acquisition and sale of assets, such as computer systems, buildings, and so forth. The board normally sets a threshold for such approvals. Depending on the size of the school, it could be as low as $1,000 or as high as $10,000.
- Hires auditor and reviews results.
- Reviews the performance of the school (financial and educational).
- Conducts annual performance appraisals of the top manager/administrator and approves any salary changes or bonuses.
- Implements annual board training and self-evaluation.
- Monitors legal compliance with licensing compliance and human resources systems.
- Assumes responsibility for crisis intervention in the event of a major event in the school.

The management team also will continue to grow as the needs require and the budget permits. One of the big challenges is to attract good management talent. The most effective source of such talent is through the network that the existing team has developed within the educational community. If other schools close or downsizing affecting administrations takes place because of budget shortfalls, excellent management talent may become available. Interviews should be structured and address the key demands of the job and the culture of the school. Open-ended questions are best to avoid leading the candidates to the desired responses. Specifically, when interviewing potential new members of the management team, the following questions should be considered:

- Does the candidate meet the needs created by current gaps in the existing team?
- Does the candidate meet the needs created by anticipated future gaps in the team?
- Will the candidate fit into the culture of the school? Does he or she share the values and beliefs of the school?

- Will the candidate share and be able to articulate the vision of the school?
- If the candidate has worked within traditional public schools, can he or she work in the entrepreneurial environment of the school?

Smaller start-up schools cannot always pay the same salaries as larger school systems. That does not mean that good candidates cannot be hired. There are factors beyond pay that can attract excellent talent, such as offering more flexibility than can a public school system with all its bureaucratic rules. For example, one residential school was able to hire a key manager for less than his current pay because the school could offer the flexibility he wanted in his work schedule. The key is to listen to each candidate's needs and try to respond in a manner that will still be considered equitable by the existing employees. The quality of the team and the mission of the school also is a nonsalary factor in some people's career choice. If the candidate is too expensive, it may be possible to bring him or her in as a consultant.

The role of advisers and consultants often will expand after the school opens. Such additional duties may include the following:

- Enhance ongoing curriculum development
- Assist in required staff training
- Serve in temporary management roles
- Assess legal and regulatory compliance
- Create and audit risk management plans
- Address employment law risks and issues
- Enhance the management development and training process

Advisory Boards

Many entrepreneurs find it beneficial to bring together a group of individuals beyond the formal board who can help provide guidance for the school and its management team. Such a group, called an *advisory board*, most often provides its advice and guidance at no charge to the school. Advisory boards have no legal authority in the operation of the school. Such a board can include various experts from inside and outside the field of education. For example, in many charter schools, the boards are typically made up primarily of teachers, administrators, and parents. The lead administrator may believe that additional expertise could help in the management of the school. He or she may bring in a group that has legal and business expertise that the management team and the board do not have among its members. The school leader should make absolutely clear to both the advisory board and the school's formal board why both exist and which has what specific roles. If managed properly, the advisory board can complement the formal board. Sometimes advisory boards can be set up as a "roundtable" of leaders from a variety of schools who can serve each other as a mutual board of advisers.

SUMMARY

The educational entrepreneur's team includes a broad range of individuals, including the management team, the board, advisers, and outside consultants. Careful assessment of the skills and talents of those within the founding group compared with those whom the school needs as it grows identifies the gaps that will need to be filled. The next chapter discusses the next major section of the business plan: the operating plan.

CHAPTER 8

The Operating Plan

The next major section of a school's business plan is its *operating plan*, which presents specific operating goals and resource needs for the school. The operating plan also details how successful operations are going to be achieved, when each step needs to be implemented, and how much each component will cost. Just as the marketing plan guides the revenue portion of the financial forecast, the operating plan guides the expense portion of the forecast. The basic components of an operating plan for a school include a facilities plan, staffing and human resource plans, a purchasing plan, a transportation plan, and plans for administrative control systems. The curricular and pedagogical plans for the school most often are specific to each school, depending on its mission, population, and regulatory requirements. Such matters are beyond the scope of this book, which has a focus on the "business side" of school start-ups. Many excellent resources are available for school founders on such matters. Therefore, this chapter focuses on the remaining components of the operating plan, which often are overlooked by school founders in their planning.

FACILITIES PLAN

Cost Factors

Other than staff payroll expenses, facility costs are the single largest expenditure for a school. Facility costs include the monthly rent or mortgage, utilities, building supplies and maintenance, and upkeep for the playground and grounds. (The terms *rent* and *lease* are used interchangeably in this chapter.) When examining facilities options, there are four main factors: cost, location, flexibility, and quality. It is important to keep in mind that while cost may seem like it should increase with the location, flexibility, and quality of the location, this is not always the case. Without careful planning, many schools end up paying too much for inferior spaces. They move too quickly to secure a location without full consideration of the terms and conditions of that space, without examining issues that can be negotiated in the lease or purchase, and without evaluations of all possible options. On the other hand, those schools that research and plan their options for space often find that they can meet acceptable or even superior flexibility and quality for comparatively lower facilities expenses. Therefore, the school founders should carefully consider each of these factors and their relative importance for them in the development of their business plan.

There are a variety of issues associated with facilities for which *flexibility* is beneficial for a school that intends to rent its facilities. Before these are examined, a brief discussion of the lease from a landlord's perspective can be helpful in understanding these issues. A landlord is generally trying to secure a predetermined return on the investment made in a building. The landlord will have a fixed set of costs that need to be covered through rent, plus some level of profit associated with the risk of owning property, which is generally much less than most people believe. Therefore, although the landlord can be flexible when renting space, there are constraints that will limit the degree of flexibility. Each negotiation should be thought of as a compromise, as each concession on the part of a landlord may create the need for some concession on the part of the tenant. Generally, the following is an outline of the areas where negotiation can take place beyond simply the rental rate charged, although each may have some impact on that rate:

- *Length of the lease:* This can vary significantly. Generally, the shorter the term of the lease (less that three years is generally considered short-term), the higher the rents and the less flexibility the school will have with the other issues that follow. A school that is willing to commit to a longer lease is generally able to negotiate more concessions in other areas. The risk of a long-term lease is that the leadership may believe that it locks the school into the space for the full term of the lease. However, it may be possible to reduce this risk, that is, to create the option to leave the space before the end of the lease through the negotiation process.

- *Renewability of the lease:* This refers to the option to extend the agreement beyond the time of the initial lease. The founders may be uncertain whether the space they are leasing will be adequate for the school in the long term. The initial term of the lease will give them the option to relocate the school if it makes sense toward the end of the initial lease. However, the right to renew under the same basic terms of the initial lease gives the option to stay if the space does in fact meet the school's needs. Typically, there can be a predetermined agreement on the increase in rent on the renewal of the lease, and the number of years the lease can be renewed to protect the school from an unexpected increase in facilities costs at the end of the first term of the lease.

- *Up-fit expenses:* These are expenses associated with finishing or renovating the internal space to meet the needs of the tenant. Depending on the space, landlords may allow a certain dollar amount per square foot, called the *up-fit allowance*, for such expense. This cost is factored into the monthly rent. Therefore, if a tenant is willing to take the space "as is," the landlord may be willing to negotiate a lower monthly rent if up-fit expenses were originally included. Any expenses to modify the space that exceed the budgeted amount are the responsibility of the tenant. For example, assume that a landlord is including an up-fit allowance of $20 per square foot on a space of 5,000 square feet for a total budget of $100,000. While this may seem like a large budget, schools often require specific features, including the number of bathroom fixtures, special exits, handicap access, and so forth, that can add up very quickly. The operating plan should identify all features required by law and all additional features that the school founders wish to have in the building. A thorough and accurate cost estimate of the features in each proposed space should be calculated to determine the actual cost to get each space up to the required and desired standards. Remember, landlords may not be accustomed to working with schools as tenants, so it is the responsibility of the school founders to identify all these requirements. For example, if the actual cost to up-fit the space is $200,000, then the tenant will have to either pay the additional $100,000 directly or try to negotiate this cost into the monthly rent. Some landlords may require a longer lease in such a case (again, everything in leases is a trade-off). When looking at multiple possible sites for a school, it is critical to look at the *total* cost of the space. One rent may seem cheaper at first glance, but that same space may have a lower allowance or may require more money to get the space up to standards. Examine the cost of the lease with all up-fit costs factored in.

- *First-year or early-months discounts:* Sometimes landlords are willing to offer discounted payments or even rent abatements for the first few months of the lease. Unless the landlord is doing this because of a weak real estate market, the tenant needs to understand that the cost of this is still factored into the total rents that will be paid over the life of the lease. Still, such terms can help a new school manage its cash flow during the first few months, when expenses can be extraordinarily high and some revenues may be delayed. For example, assume that a new private school will open in the fall. The team will need to move in during the summer to set up the school and to allow time to hire and train staff. Since tuition will not start coming into the school until some time after the school's opening, an abatement of rent during the summer may be a significant benefit by preserving scarce cash.
- *Inflation risk:* Most leases have some form of annual increase built into them. There may be a single adjustment, or there may be separate adjustments for the base rent and general building expenses (such as shared utilities and common ground maintenance). Such adjustments can be predetermined, tied to a specified measure of inflation, or based on documented costs incurred for the building. The school leaders may wish to have a predictable fixed increase, but this will come at a cost. Most landlords will set this increase higher than what may actually occur to ensure that any unforeseen increases or bursts of inflation are covered with the increase in rent.
- *Expandability:* This is an issue that can be negotiated in a lease at a predetermined rate or rate formula. A school may request the option to take on additional space or grounds as the school grows and

may exercise its right to take on the additional space at any time. The landlord will reserve the right to lease the space to another tenant but will give the school what is known as a *right of first refusal*. Usually, the landlord will reserve the right to lease the space or grounds to another tenant if the school does not act within a rather short period of time.

- *Assignment:* A school may wish to negotiate the right to sublease its space, called an *assignment*, to another tenant. The landlord will likely have the right to veto the new tenant if it does meet certain standards. Generally, the school is still responsible for the lease but is given the option to cover the costs through the sublease. This allows for a school to move out of a building before the end of the lease.

- *Cancellation penalties:* These are clearly defined in most leases. Although the tenant will have the right to terminate a lease before it is completed, the landlord can impose a financial penalty for doing so. Without such a clause in a lease, the tenant is legally liable for all the payments for the entire term of the lease. The penalty will be set at an amount that is more than enough to cover the estimated cost of the time it will take to get a new tenant in place and to cover any incidental costs that will likely be incurred, such as the legal costs associated with drafting the new lease.

The *quality* of the space is generally determined by the age of the space and the types of materials used in construction and up-fit. Most schools do not need the highest grade of quality. It is helpful to look at space with varying degrees of quality to determine what level is required for the school. Although a lower level of quality may be perfectly acceptable for the school, the durability of the materials used in construction should be considered, as children are much harder on space than one would experience in an average office building.

Location can drive the cost of space significantly, depending on convenience, traffic flow, safety, neighborhood conditions, and general demand in that specific area. Some location factors that typically drive up cost, such as visibility or proximity to major commuter routes, may not be critically important for a school. In fact, a location away from major routes closer to a residential area may be desirable.

However, location also is directly correlated to transportation costs, so both should be evaluated together.

Finding Space

The process of finding the best space for a new school can take several months. A systematic approach can help make the probability of success within the desired time frame higher:

1. *Develop a detailed facilities specification for the school:* The specifications should include number of classrooms, size of rooms, office space, playground space, proximity to the target market, cafeteria space, gymnasium space, and so forth and should be detailed and comprehensive. Each specific component or the degree to which each component is satisfied should be rated as critical, important, or desirable. For example, it may be decided that the minimum size for each classroom of 400 square feet is critical because the law mandates this. However, the nature of the school's programs makes it important to have a minimum size of at least 500 square feet, and the teachers believe that at least 600 square feet per classroom is *desirable* to accomplish their pedagogical objectives.

2. *Identify a real estate expert to work with the school:* A real estate agent should be used to identify possible sites on the basis of the facility specifications. Given the unique needs of a school, the team also should work to identify possible sites. For example, an unused school building tied to a church's campus may be something that the agent is not aware of but that can be identified through networking with other educational professionals and community leaders.

3. *Create a list of optional locations:* If financially possible, look at a variety of options, including leasing and purchasing facilities for the school. The specification list will narrow the options considerably, so within that list it is important to remain as flexible as possible. The options for space are as follows:
   - *Rent "as is":* By renting a property "as is," the rent charged can be kept to a minimum, and a lease can be made fairly short-term. The main disadvantage is that the space may not

meet all the regulatory and programmatic requirements of the school.

- *Rent or buy a site that requires modest modifications of the existing space:* In this scenario, the basic structural nature of the building is left as is, such as walls, windows, plumbing, heating, and so forth. Any modifications are more cosmetic, such as wall coverings and floor coverings, although some minor construction also can be undertaken, such as dividing a large room with a new wall or taking down a wall to create a larger room out of two smaller ones. While this approach will allow for a better fit with the specifications of the school, it will also increase the cost of the space, as the cost of modifying the space will be added into the rent or the cost of the mortgage.

- *Rent or construct a new building:* Generally, new construction costs more than existing buildings. Therefore, a new building for a school will be more expensive than simply modifying existing space. In addition, new construction will take longer to get ready. Existing space will normally take thirty to ninety days to make ready for occupancy, while new construction will often take six to twelve months to complete.

- *Renovation:* While it may seem exciting to renovate an older building, particularly one that has a certain charm or historic significance, keep in mind that this can be the most complex and by far the most expensive option. Renovation usually requires extensive retrofitting of wiring, plumbing, and heating and major changes in the actual structure of the building, which is very expensive to accomplish up to the standards required for school buildings.

4. *Evaluate the options on the basis of cost and features:* Create a spreadsheet to thoroughly evaluate every option and compare all these to the ideal set of specifications already identified.

5. *Use all members of the team to assess the final options:* The management team, board members, and advisers all bring perspectives that can help ensure that all issues are completely evaluated. This decision is too important to make without a general consensus that the best possible space is chosen.

If acceptable space is not identified, it may be possible to find a short-term option for the school. Clearly this is not the best option, as the space may not meet many important specifications, and a move, even during the summer, can be very disruptive. However, sometimes it is the only option. For example, Academia Cesar Chavez in St. Paul, Minnesota, had planned to move into space near the predominantly Hispanic West Side neighborhood. No space could be found in that part of St. Paul that met specifications. Through networking with educational professionals, an unused Catholic school building was located. The only problem was that it was several miles from the West Side and, worst yet, across the Mississippi River (a psychological barrier in the city). Although the distance would create a barrier for enrollment, it was the only location that would work and still allow the school to open in time. A short-term (two-year) lease was negotiated, and the staff continued to search and plan for more permanent space closer to their target market. Very few modifications to the building were needed, so both the church and the school could agree on an acceptable lease contract.

Neighborhood Relations

Although it is typically said that "schools make good neighbors," many private schools bring in children from other neighborhoods, have a specific mission or religious affiliation, or even work with troubled or marginalized children. Even under the best of circumstances, neighborhood relations can be difficult for the new school because of increased traffic. Therefore, the operating plan should include a neighborhood relations component that addresses the need to develop a good relationship during planning, start-up, and growth of the school. During the planning phase, neighborhood meetings or forums should be set up to provide accurate information about the school and a chance for neighbors to give their input into the planning process. For example, the founders of a residential school for boys with minor to moderate behavioral problems being planned in the rural Southeast discovered that a few neighbors who did not want the school in their area under any circumstances had begun to spread rumors. The word in the community was that the school was going to house criminally insane youth. The founders quickly planned a series of neighborhood meetings to provide accurate information and allow for citizens to raise any concerns that they had about the school. By the third meeting, only the handful of neighbors who had started the rumors showed up. The rest of the neighbors were satisfied with the information they received, and many actually expressed a desire to volunteer at the school once it opened.

During start-up, it is good public relations to hold an open house for neighbors to come in and visit the new school. Even though most schools find that only a small percentage of neighbors will attend the open house, just the fact that an open house was held and the neighbors were invited creates a great deal of goodwill. During the start-up, the neighbors should be supplied with contact information so they can easily reach the leadership team with any questions, concerns, or ideas about the operation of the school.

Once the school is operational, it is good to host periodic neighborhood meetings, usually at least once per school year. If newsletters or other communications are generated for parents, they also can be distributed to neighbors to keep them informed of developments in the school.

Other Facilities Expenses

A major part of the facilities cost of a school can be the heating and cooling of the building, especially the larger spaces such as the gymnasium and cafeteria. Policies and procedures should be developed that ensure that heating and cooling is done as efficiently as possible. For example, in very warm climates, it may be possible to start school earlier in the day to avoid having to fully cool the buildings during the hottest part of the day. Even the calendar may be modified to work with the seasonal changes in temperatures and reduce heating and cooling expenses.

The upkeep and maintenance of the school also should be planned for. Schools can hire their own staff, contract with a landlord, or contract with an outside company for part or all of the maintenance functions. During the planning phase, the cost of all options should be examined to make certain that the expense forecasts are as accurate as possible and that the most cost-effective options are chosen.

STAFFING AND HUMAN RESOURCE PLANS

The single largest expense in any school is employee costs, which include salaries, benefits, and bonuses. In a start-up school, there are two dimensions to employee expense: the number of staff and the timing of the hiring of staff. Both must be carefully considered to ensure that cash flow is not unnecessarily strained during the early growth of the school. This is referred to as the *staffing plan*. Once employees are beginning to be hired, the school should develop systems to effectively recruit, select, and evaluate its employees. This is known as the school's *human resource plan.*

Staffing Plan

Effectively forecasting the number of employees that a school will need requires that the leadership team work within a number of constraints. This is where significant debate may occur within the leadership of the school. Those whose focus on the quality of education will push for smaller classes, more staff in each classroom, and a higher number of general educational support staff. Those whose focus is on the financial management of the school will bring into the discussion the reality of what the budget will allow. In a public school setting, this battle often is played out in more of a negotiating framework. That is, each side has the capacity to give a little bit. In a start-up school, the cash that is available is all that there is to work with, so it becomes important to have the entire leadership team work together to arrive at a workable and affordable staffing plan. Unfortunately, many educators are engrained in the negotiating framework from years of working in public schools. To achieve real consensus, all members of the leadership team must have full information of all the constraints. Although the process will be iterative, it should be based on movement toward consensus, not compromise:

1. Begin with the basic assumptions about class size and number of classrooms. At this point, those with a focus on the academics of the school should create their "reasonable" model. Never start with an "ideal" model, as start-up schools almost never have the

resources to meet this type of scenario. By starting from a realistic point, it is much easier to reach consensus.

2. Make assumptions about the number of educational support staff per classroom. Again, the goal is to make a "reasonable" model, understanding that it may have to change, depending on constraints.

3. Create a schedule that estimates the salary of each type of staff (teacher, classroom aide, reading specialist, special education teacher, and so forth). Remember to add on about 30 percent to base salaries to cover the cost of benefits (employer portion of social security, health insurance, unemployment insurance, and so forth). This percentage may be higher or lower in different markets, so if a more accurate estimate of benefits is known, use that figure instead.

4. Develop a spreadsheet that begins to forecast the total cost required for the academic staff of the school.

5. Estimate the staffing requirements of the administrative unit of the school, including the administrator, the business manager, food service, custodial, and so forth. Again, develop a schedule of expected salaries for these staff and a spreadsheet that shows total estimated costs.

6. Create a priority ranking of all staff. Each position should be rated as essential, important, or desirable. This ranking is critical as staffing plans are adjusted up and down to reflect changing projections and budgets.

The dimension of timing must now be considered by creating a month-by-month spreadsheet that shows estimated cash flow into the school each month on the top and an estimate of when each of the staff will need to be hired and the total cost of this staff underneath. Although negative cash flow should be expected before the school is operating, once students are registered and cash is flowing in for those children, the school needs to be covering its operating expenses. A major challenge that schools have is that employees are generally hired at the beginning of the academic year. In other organizations, employees can be hired throughout the year. Many schools find that this may require postponement of some hirings until the second year.

Once estimated revenues and staff expenses are entered into the spreadsheet, it should become clear whether any initial adjustments to the staffing plan are required. Generally, total employee costs in a school should average about 60 to 65 percent of the total revenues. The remaining 35 to 40 percent will be used to pay rent, classroom supplies, textbooks, meals, and so forth. If the date from this initial spreadsheet falls within these general guidelines, no further action is required at this time. However, when the complete financial forecast and budget are prepared (see chapter 9), adjustments in the staffing plan may be required. Table 8.1 displays a sample format for the staffing plan spreadsheet.

In this very simple example, the spreadsheet shows revenues received from tuition and grants totaling $120,000 per month. The staffing plan has an increase in employees during the summer until full staffing is in place by the beginning of school. Benefits are assumed to cost 30 percent of salaries. In this example, the percentage of employee expenses to revenues is $104,000/$120,000, or 86.7 percent. This is much higher than the 60 to 65 percent average for most schools. Therefore, the leadership team should meet to determine what changes can be made in the staffing plan. Can classes be larger? Can classrooms share teacher aides? Can the hiring of certain educational specialists be postponed until the second year? Can administrative staffing be cut by expanding people's duties? For example, the lead administrator could be assigned to perform the duties of the business manager for the first year, or the school may need to get by without a full-time receptionist. Even once the staffing plan is in alignment

Table 8.1.   Sample Staffing Plan Spreadsheet

	July	August	September	October	Etc.
Estimated revenues					
Tuition	0	0	100,000	100,000	
Grants	20,000	20,000	20,000	20,000	
Total revenues	20,000	20,000	120,000	120,000	
Salaries	50,000	60,000	80,000	80,000	
Benefits	15,000	18,000	24,000	24,000	
Total employee expenses	65,000	78,000	104,000	104,000	
Percent			86.7%	86.7%	

with the estimated revenues, the leadership must keep in mind that it may need further refinement as the full financial forecast is developed. This may suggest that further staff may need to be cut or that some who were cut in this initial stage may be able to be reinstated into the plan. Therefore, the team must agree on clear priorities of all the possible staff positions in the plan.

Human Resource Plan

The recruitment, selection, and performance evaluation processes are the components of a human resource plan. Some new businesses can develop these processes over time, as hiring often is very slow during the first year or two. In a school, a core of employees must be in place from the very beginning, including teachers, administrators, and support staff. Therefore, it is a sound management practice to have adequate human resource systems in place from the start of operations. In addition, licensing and sponsorship requirements dictate the need for human resource systems.

Mathew Metz, principal of St. Ambrose Catholic School in Woodbury, Minnesota, stresses the need for planning in the recruitment process:

> To avoid some of the challenges that are usually associated with starting a school, we did some planning up front. We offered a well-put-together compensation package to attract good staff. We wanted staff that believed in the Catholic education system, and so we advertised that at St. Ambrose they could make a living teaching but also keep the Catholic school system values. This helped us attract over 600 applicants for twenty-four positions.

Effective recruitment and selection systems consider more than just the technical aspects of each position. Evaluation of each candidate's ability to perform the job within the specific environment of the school and within its culture should be given equal consideration. For example, a school for emotionally troubled children will require teachers who are much more than well-trained educators. Teachers also must be able to work within the stress and disruption that such a student body can create in the classroom. That is the *environment* in which the job is performed. Furthermore, the school will have a culture that dictates how children, parents, other staff, and outside stakeholders are to be treated. The teacher must have a style and a belief structure that fit within the school's culture. All three factors—skill, environment, and culture—must be considered when evaluating each potential employee. A teacher who meets just one or two of these factors is likely to fail. Recruitment and selection processes should clearly and honestly reflect all three areas realistically. It does no one any good to gloss over the environment and culture of a school just to hire a technically good teacher.

The performance evaluation process also should reflect all three of these areas. Is the teacher an effective educator? Is the teacher working effectively within the environment of the school? Does the teacher embrace the norms and beliefs of the school? These three questions should guide the evaluation process not only of teachers but of all employees in the school as well.

The operating plan should explicitly address guidelines that will shape the development of the human resource systems of the new school. The formal employee handbook and manuals that will put all these guidelines into practice are developed by the management team and approved by the board, preferably before the school opens. Some schools put the finishing touches on these documents after the first school year begins, but in no case should this extend beyond the first year of operation.

PURCHASING PLAN

A purchasing plan should be included in the operating plan. The *purchasing plan* will provide a summary of how materials are ordered, including forms, procedures, and so forth. It will provide a detailed schedule of who has spending authority for what types of purchases and in what amounts. The plan prescribes what limits there are on the purchasing authority of various positions in the school (such as the top administrator, supervisors, teachers, and so forth). Inventory policies should be carefully thought through. Although it may be more convenient to keep large inventories on hand, such purchases can lead to waste and can use up precious cash. Policies on gifts from suppliers should be explicitly spelled out. The best approach is to adopt strict policies that allow for accepting no gifts from any suppliers unless those gifts benefit the entire school and not just the individual making the purchase.

Food purchasing should have specific attention in the purchasing plan. The mismanagement of food can amount to large sums of wasted resources. Food costs are most likely to be unnecessarily increased through waste (unused or uneaten food) and employee theft. Although larger purchases can bring down the cost through volume discounts offered by suppliers, this will increase the likelihood of waste and increase the cost of storage. Benchmarks for food cost are easily obtained by industry groups and should be used to manage the staff responsible for meals. Many schools find that using outside vendors to supply meals for the children can reduce expenses significantly. The relative cost of preparing meals with the school's staff should be compared with the cost of outsourcing these services. Existing schools are a good source of data to make such a comparison and to get references for food vendors.

TRANSPORTATION PLAN

Some schools, such as charter schools in certain states, are required by statute to provide transportation. Typically when it is mandated, there is funding to support the costs. Such funding is on a per child basis, so it may not cover all the costs of transportation. There are still significant logistical and operational issues to consider. How far can children effectively be bused to the school? How dispersed an area can busing be supported? It may be possible for charter schools to utilize public school buses. However, that may mean that the school will need to be flexible about operating hours, as the same buses are used on a staggered basis for public school transportation. If a private company is used, the operating plan should make specific assumptions about busing requirements so that potential busing companies can make accurate forecasts of this expense.

For private schools, transportation is not mandated but may be a marketing issue. That is, there may be some expectation of transportation among parents in the market. Market research should investigate this issue to make certain that there is a clear understanding of the parents' expectations. There may be a middle ground in which transportation can be coordinated, possibly for a fee. Options may include subcontracting transportation with a private company or even developing a system for facilitating ride share among families. Whatever is decided, careful planning of the real cost and requirements of transportation is essential, as many schools have underestimated the cost of this critical item.

ADMINISTRATIVE CONTROL SYSTEMS

The budgeting process is the heart of the administrative control systems of a school. The first-year budget is the most difficult, as there are no historical data to use to estimate revenues and expenses. Nonetheless, the school must have systems in place to effectively manage the cash flow. Budgets should be considered fluid documents in a start-up. If revenues fall short of projections, expenses need to be cut to ensure that the school is able to survive. This is one of the most difficult adjustments for those who have worked in public schools, where the mentality is that if it is budgeted, it can be spent. In a freestanding school, budgeted dollars can be spent only if the projected cash actually comes into the school to cover those expenses. Chapter 9 discusses cash management in more detail. Suffice it to say that spending and expense reimbursement must be a day-to-day concern in a start-up school, and every employee should have knowledge and ownership of the process.

SUMMARY

The operating plan includes a careful examination of facilities, staffing, purchasing, transportation, and administrative control systems. The quality of the operating plan and its assumptions will dictate the accuracy of the expense forecasts and budgets in the business plan. The next chapter integrates the revenue and expense forecasts discussed thus far into a financial plan that will provide documentation for financing and will help guide the start-up and early operation of the school.

CHAPTER 9

The Financial Plan

The past several chapters have detailed the process of developing the assumptions that underlie accurate revenue and expense forecasts. All these chapters presented various steps culminating in the development of a business plan for a school. In this chapter, all this is integrated to create the financial forecasts and budgets for a start-up school, which is the final step in the business planning process. Financial forecasting is iterative. Adjustments will need to be made in the revenue and expense projections to ensure that the school has a sound and balanced budget. Specific aspects of the financing of a school may require outside funding, but a major goal of the forecasting process should be to minimize the need for debt or other financing.

FINANCIAL PROJECTIONS

Accurate revenue forecasts depend on the quality of the research used to develop the marketing plan. Bankers and private investors review dozens or even hundreds of business plans every year. When reviewing a plan, most start with the same first step. These experts carefully examine how well the marketing plan explains the revenue lines in the financial projections. They are looking for the internal logic that creates the backbone of a good business plan. In a school, there are three aspects of the revenue forecasts that should be explained by the marketing plan:

1. *Enrollments:* Market research should have given an estimate of the total population of children who fit into the target market

of the school. From this, the marketing plan should have presented clear steps on how the school will address the needs of this population. From that, an assumption must be made as to what percentage of the target population is expected to enroll. If models are available from other schools or, better yet, if hard data of intended enrollments from potential customers can be included in the plan, this can help strengthen the argument for proposed enrollment estimates. Ramona Rosales, executive director of Academia Cesar Chavez in St. Paul, Minnesota, stated, "We turned to the Minnesota Association of Charter Schools to figure out the revenue piece. We obtained another template from the association in which we started inputting numbers on grade levels and how many students."

As a general rule, the higher the percentage assumed, the less credible the plan becomes to potential funders, such as bankers or foundations. Funders realize that moving children from established schools to a new school is a difficult decision that families do not take lightly, so it is logical that the percentage who are willing to do this will be fairly low.

2. *Tuition or per pupil payments:* Projected tuition or per pupil payments should be strongly supported in the marketing plan. It is not unusual to see schools using pricing assumptions in their forecasts that have little justification. For tuition, comparable market rates and value should guide the figures used in the model.

3. *Grants and fund-raising:* There are a variety of grants and other sources of fund-raising that can offset some of the costs of a new school. Some grants are one-time in nature and are meant to support start-up expenses such as textbooks, computers, playground equipment, and so forth. Other grants may help offset salaries that must be paid before tuition or other payments begin to flow into the school. Market research should include an investigation of sources of external funding from foundations and other granting agencies before the start-up of the school. Significant commitments for funding can be secured during the planning phase, but it will require an effective business plan presentation to the right group willing to support the mission of the school.

No matter how good the available market data or other information for the plan are, assumptions will have to be made in constructing the revenue forecast. These assumptions should be documented, as they will become an important part of the management of the start-up school. If assumptions prove to be inaccurate, the leadership team will need to adjust the budget midyear to account for any shortfalls or surpluses. Assumptions may include the percentage of the target market that actually enrolls, the balance in enrollments among the various grade levels offered by the school, the amount of grants available, the number of children on school-sponsored scholarships, and so forth.

As introduced in chapter 4, financial forecasts should start from an assumed level of excess cash flow for the school and not just toward breakeven. In the beginning of the school, the excess cash flow will likely be used to make payments against loans that helped fund start-up. Over time, the surplus cash flow is used to build modest yet critical cash reserves for unexpected or emergency needs or to serve as a foundation for future capital needs, such as building expansion.

A start-up school should be continuously testing enrollment estimates as it prepares to open. Commitments for enrollment, through applications or enrollment deposits, can be a barometer for actual enrollments weeks or even a few months before the school opens. For example, assume that Morningside School has revenue forecasts that are based on enrollments of 300 children. This is based on an assumption of two classes of twenty-five children in each of six grade levels. In June, the school begins to take applications and enrollment deposits. From talking with other schools in their community, the founders were told that for most independent schools about 25 percent of students enroll in June, 25 percent in July, and 50 percent in August (note that these are not generalizable figures for all start-up schools and are used for illustration purposes only). At the end of June, Morningside School had the following commitments:

	Actual	Projected
Kindergarten	18	13
First grade	12	13
Second grade	14	13
Third grade	10	13
Fourth grade	7	13
Fifth grade	5	13

This data concerned the management team, who recognized a crucial need to increase their marketing efforts. But more fundamentally, they realized that their assumptions were not correct. It was very likely that they would be able to fill only one class of fourth and fifth grades and that the third grade was somewhat in doubt. In addition, they needed to make a decision as to whether to cap the number of kindergarten students at fifty, let those classes get a little larger to offset the lower numbers in other levels, or even open a third classroom. As tempting as the second two choices were from a financial perspective, the team decided that they would create problems in future years by accepting too many kindergarten students this year.

In July, the following commitments were in place:

	Actual	Projected
Kindergarten	35	25
First grade	23	25
Second grade	27	25
Third grade	15	25
Fourth grade	14	13
Fifth grade	12	13

The lower projections for fourth and fifth grade reflected the decision in June to cut back to one classroom for each grade level. At this point, the management team decided to cut back to a single classroom of third grade as well. This led them to reconsider their decision on the kindergarten classes. With some flexibility in their use of facilities, they decided that they could accommodate a third kindergarten class. Without the additional students, the overall financial situation of Morningside School might come into serious trouble. Had the management team not tracked these assumptions and used them to make decisions about the start-up of the school, it may not have had enough cash flow to survive the first year. Classes were eliminated even before all the teachers were hired. This scenario is based on actual data compiled from several start-up schools.

This example illustrates the importance of identifying and measuring assumptions. In this example, there were assumptions about when commitments for enrollments occur over the summer, the balance of enrollments across the grade levels, and the number of classes per grade level that the school could effectively manage. The school tested these assumptions each month. In fact, all assumptions should be tested in this way at whatever predetermined milestone makes sense. These tests can, such as in this example, be based on time as well as on enrollments, revenues, number of classes, some key event, or some other milestone that seems reasonable for the assumption being evaluated.

Many schools rely on some form of *accounts receivable* for the revenue charged. That is, parents or funding agencies enroll children and make a commitment to pay for those children. Payment rarely occurs at the time of service as it would in a retail business. Instead, there is an implied or possibly explicit contract that commits the customer to pay within some specified period of time. For example, assume that a school charges tuition by the month. Generally, the school expects payment in full at the beginning of each month, but some families may not always pay on time. This creates an account receivable from that family. The business office of the school must monitor and manage these accounts receivable. The school's budget assumes that cash is flowing in each month to cover the expenses, but if too many families get too far behind in their payments, this can create a serious cash flow problem for the school. A certain level of late payments should be built into the cash flow projections for the school to allow for this inevitable event. This creates yet another assumption: The percentage of tuition that is paid one or two months late needs to be monitored and managed so that late tuition can more effectively be collected.

Expense Forecasting

As discussed in chapter 2, there are two basic types of costs: fixed and variable. *Fixed* costs are those that remain the same no matter what the level of enrollments in the school. Facility rent is a good example of a fixed cost. As a general rule, it is advisable to keep fixed costs as low as possible. Therefore, the lower the fixed costs are, the less of a burden it is to pay these costs if enrollments are low. *Variable* costs are those that vary directly with the enrollments of the school. An example of a variable cost is food costs, as the number of meals prepared varies with enrollment. Not all costs fit neatly into one of these two basic categories. Some costs are mixed; that is, they have a fixed portion and a portion that varies. For example, phone costs include a fixed monthly charge per line plus a variable charge for long-distance usage. Step costs do not increase smoothly with each additional student, such as in a variable cost like food, but do increase at certain intervals. Teacher salaries are the most common example of this in a school. This cost increases each time a classroom is added, which is dependent on enrollment thresholds (for example, for every twenty-five students, a classroom is added and another teacher is hired). The nature of each category of expense must be understood to develop an accurate model when forecasting expenses.

In general, a good place to begin developing an expense forecast for a new school is by starting with expense histories of schools already operating. Generally, many school administrators are more than willing to share some or all of their expense data:

> We obtained a template from the National Council of La Razas, which laid out generally what charter schools cost to run. After formulating our own costs around the template, we visited an existing charter school to answer more of our questions on costs. (Ramona Rosales, executive director, Academia Cesar Chavez, St. Paul, Minnesota)

Just as with revenues, expense forecasts require a certain number of assumptions when planning a new school. The most significant revolve around salaries and benefits. What will teacher pay actually be? Although historical market data are available, market conditions can create changes from year to year that could alter the cost structure of a school. How much will benefits actually cost? Reasonable estimates can be made, but health care cost increases have been unpredictable for the past several years, seeing sudden spikes of double-digit increases. Even the cost of the facility is only an estimate until the lease is actually signed, and the business plan will need to be developed well before this event. All assumptions for expenses should be added to the list of revenue assumptions, as they too will be important management tools. This list should include how the assumptions will be measured and at what time intervals these measures will be evaluated.

INTEGRATING AND ADJUSTING THE
FORECASTED FINANCIAL STATEMENTS

For a start-up school, the single most important financial statement is one that forecasts not just the revenues and expenses but also the actual projected month-by-month cash flow. When integrating the revenue and expense forecasts into a single statement, this is the first test of that overall model. Tables 9.1 through 9.3 display an example of such an integrated statement for the first six months of a hypothetical new school. In practice, two full years should be included, but this will suffice for the purposes of the current discussion. Note that in all three scenarios, the budget includes one-time expenditures for supplies and furnishings for the start-up of the school.

Three different versions of the financial statements are presented. Table 9.1 displays a cash flow budget based on what are considered optimistic assumptions related to the revenues for this school. It is assumed that enrollments will generate $190,500 in tuition, which means the school is at about 90 percent of its capacity. It also is assumed that the school will be awarded a $250,000 start-up grant and $5,000 per month in other fund-raising. Table 9.2 is the conservative set of assumptions regarding revenues. In this scenario, enrollments are at about 80 percent of capacity, the start-up grant is for $200,000, and fund-raising yields only $2,500 per month. In the final scenario, table 9.3 shows the worst-case set of assumptions. This scenario assumes that no grant is received, that no fund-raising takes place, and that the school is only at about two-thirds of its capacity. The potential scenarios are endless, but these are three that, in the minds of the management team, represent varying sets of assumptions that make sense to evaluate in order to understand the impact on the cash needs of the school.

In the optimistic scenario, the school will need to secure $111,414 in additional funding if all the assumptions prove to be exactly correct. This number can be seen in the very bottom line of table 9.1, which is the ending cash balance. Since this is the largest negative number during the start-up, it represents the highest shortfall the school will face. As the ending cash balance gets higher (smaller negative numbers) each month after August, this indicates that the school is generating

Table 9.1. Sample Six-Month Operational Cash Flow Budget for New School: Optimistic Assumptions

	July	August	September	October	November	December
Beginning cash balance	0	7,793	−111,414	−75,452	−39,489	−3,526
Revenues						
Tuition			190,500	190,500	190,500	190,500
Start-up grants	250,000					
Fees:						
food service			16,000	16,000	16,000	16,000
Other fund-raising	5,000	5,000	5,000	5,000	5,000	5,000
Total receipts	255,000	5,000	211,500	211,500	211,500	211,500
Expenses						
Personnel salaries and benefits						
Salaries	88,917	88,917	88,917	88,917	88,917	88,917
Other benefits	24,008	24,008	24,008	24,008	24,008	24,008
Substitute services			1,080	1,080	1,080	1,080
Professional Development/ training	5,000	5,000	1,500	1,500	1,500	1,500
Subtotal: personnel costs	117,924	117,924	115,504	115,504	115,504	115,504
Personnel to revenue (%)			55%	55%	55%	55%
Direct student costs						

	July	August	September	October	November	December
Textbooks	40,000					
Student supplies and materials	25,000					
Curriculum materials	10,000					
Library and media center materials			500	500	500	500
Computers and materials			1,750	1,750	1,750	1,750
Classroom furnishings and supplies	51,000					
Subtotal: direct student costs	126,000	0	2,250	2,250	2,250	2,250
Facilities expenses						
Rent/lease/financing costs			30,000	30,000	30,000	30,000
Maintenance: equipment/supplies/repairs			1,000	1,000	1,000	1,000
Utilities			2,000	2,000	2,000	2,000
Subtotal: occupancy expenses		0	33,000	33,000	33,000	33,000
Administrative expenses						

(continued)

Table 9.1. Sample Six-Month Operational Cash Flow Budget for New School: Optimistic Assumptions *(continued)*

	July	August	September	October	November	December
Office supplies and materials			2,400	2,400	2,400	2,400
Office furnishings and equipment			2,000	2,000	2,000	2,000
Telephone/ telecommuni- cations	500	500	500	500	500	500
Subtotal office expenses	500	500	4,900	4,900	4,900	4,900
General expenses						
Insurance			700	700	700	700
Interest expense						
Transportation: students			400	400	400	400
Food service			16,000	16,000	16,000	16,000
Management fee	1,950	1,950	1,950	1,950	1,950	1,950
Board training		3,000				
Public relations, promotion, and marketing	833	833	833	833	833	833
Subtotal general expenses	2,783	5,783	19,883	19,883	19,883	19,883
Total nonpersonnel costs	129,283	6,283	60,033	60,033	60,033	60,033
Total costs	247,207	124,207	175,537	175,537	175,537	175,537
Ending cash balance	7,793	−111,414	−75,452	−39,489	−3,526	32,437

Table 9.2. Sample Six-Month Operational Cash Flow Budget for New School: Conservative Assumptions

	July	August	September	October	November	December
Beginning cash balance	0	–44,707	–166,414	–148,452	–130,489	–112,526
Revenues						
Tuition			175,000	175,000	175,000	175,000
Start-up grants	200,000					
Fees: food service			16,000	16,000	16,000	16,000
Other fund-raising	2,500	2,500	2,500	2,500	2,500	2,500
Total receipts	202,500	2,500	193,500	193,500	193,500	193,500
Expenses						
Personnel salaries and benefits						
Salaries	88,917	88,917	88,917	88,917	88,917	88,917
Other benefits	24,008	24,008	24,008	24,008	24,008	24,008
Substitute services			1,080	1,080	1,080	1,080
Professional development/ training	5,000	5,000	1,500	1,500	1,500	1,500
Subtotal: personnel costs	117,924	117,924	115,504	115,504	115,504	115,504
Personnel to revenue (%)			60%	60%	60%	60%
Direct student costs						
Textbooks	40,000					

(continued)

Table 9.2. Sample Six-Month Operational Cash Flow Budget for New School: Conservative Assumptions (continued)

	July	August	September	October	November	December
Student supplies and materials	25,000					
Curriculum materials	10,000					
Library and media center materials			500	500	500	500
Computers and materials			1,750	1,750	1,750	1,750
Classroom furnishings and supplies	51,000					
Subtotal: direct student costs	126,000	0	2,250	2,250	2,250	2,250
Facilities expenses						
Rent/lease/financing costs			30,000	30,000	30,000	30,000
Maintenance: equipment/supplies/repairs			1,000	1,000	1,000	1,000
Utilities			2,000	2,000	2,000	2,000
Subtotal: occupancy expenses		0	33,000	33,000	33,000	33,000
Administrative expenses						
Office supplies and materials			2,400	2,400	2,400	2,400

	July	August	September	October	November	December
Office furnishings and equipment			2,000	2,000	2,000	2,000
Telephone/telecommunications	500	500	500	500	500	500
Subtotal office expenses	500	500	4,900	4,900	4,900	4,900
General expenses						
Insurance			700	700	700	700
Interest expense						
Transportation: students			400	400	400	400
Food service	1,950		16,000	16,000	16,000	16,000
Management fee		1,950	1,950	1,950	1,950	1,950
Board training		3,000				
Public relations, promotion, and marketing	833	833	833	833	833	833
Subtotal general expenses	2,783	5,783	19,883	19,883	19,883	19,883
Total nonpersonnel costs	129,283	6,283	60,033	60,033	60,033	60,033
Total costs	247,207	124,207	175,537	175,537	175,537	175,537
Ending cash balance	−44,707	−166,414	−148,452	−130,489	−112,526	−94,563

Table 9.3. Sample Six-Month Operational Cash Flow Budget for New School: Worst-Case Assumptions

	July	August	September	October	November	December
Beginning cash balance	0	–247,207	–371,414	–390,452	–409,489	–428,526
Revenues						
Tuition			140,500	140,500	140,500	140,500
Start-up grants						
Fees: food service			16,000	16,000	16,000	16,000
Other fund-raising						
Total receipts	0	0	156,500	156,500	156,500	156,500
Expenses						
Personnel salaries and benefits						
Salaries	88,917	88,917	88,917	88,917	88,917	88,917
Other benefits	24,008	24,008	24,008	24,008	24,008	24,008
Substitute services			1,080	1,080	1,080	1,080
Professional development/ training	5,000	5,000	1,500	1,500	1,500	1,500
Subtotal: personnel costs	117,924	117,924	115,504	115,504	115,504	115,504
Personnel to revenue (%)			74%	74%	74%	74%
Direct student costs						
Textbooks	40,000					

	July	August	September	October	November	December
Student supplies and materials	25,000					
Curriculum materials	10,000					
Library and media center materials			500	500	500	500
Computers and materials			1,750	1,750	1,750	1,750
Classroom furnishings and supplies	51,000					
Subtotal: direct student costs	126,000	0	2,250	2,250	2,250	2,250
Facilities expenses						
Rent/lease/ financing costs			30,000	30,000	30,000	30,000
Maintenance: equipment/ supplies/repairs			1,000	1,000	1,000	1,000
Utilities			2,000	2,000	2,000	2,000
Subtotal: occupancy expenses	0	0	33,000	33,000	33,000	33,000
Administrative expenses						
Office supplies and materials			2,400	2,400	2,400	2,400
Office furnishings and equipment			2,000	2,000	2,000	2,000

(continued)

Table 9.3. Sample Six-Month Operational Cash Flow Budget for New School: Worst-Case Assumptions (continued)

	July	August	September	October	November	December
Telephone/ telecommuni- cations	500	500	500	500	500	500
Subtotal office expenses	500	500	4,900	4,900	4,900	4,900
General expenses						
Insurance			700	700	700	700
Interest expense						
Transportation: students			400	400	400	400
Food service	1,950	1,950	16,000	16,000	16,000	16,000
Management fee		3,000	1,950	1,950	1,950	1,950
Board training						
Public relations, promotion, and marketing	833	833	833	833	833	833
Subtotal general expenses	2,783	5,783	19,883	19,883	19,883	19,883
Total nonpersonnel costs	129,283	6,283	60,033	60,033	60,033	60,033
Total costs	247,207	124,207	175,537	175,537	175,537	175,537
Ending cash balance	−247,207	−371,414	−390,452	−409,489	−428,526	−447,563

positive cash flow each month after August. That makes sense, as tuition and fees are beginning to come in and nearly all the high start-up costs, such as books and furnishings, have been purchased. Since forecasting is never an exact science, it is best to round up the estimated cash need a little higher and assume that the school should raise $115,000. Although this scenario shows a financially healthy school, it is never advisable to use an optimistic scenario for planning and particularly not for securing outside funding. Entrepreneurs are always overly optimistic, so it is important to step back and consider a more conservative set of assumptions.

In the conservative scenario, the school will need to secure $166,414 in additional funding if all the assumptions prove to be exactly correct. This number can be seen in the very bottom line of table 9.2, which again displays the ending cash balance for each month. A modest change in assumptions—10 percent lower enrollments and fewer grants and fund-raising—has resulted in the need for about $55,000 more in outside funding beyond the start-up grant. Just as in the previous scenario, the ending cash balance gets higher (smaller negative numbers) each month after August, which indicates that the school is generating positive cash flow each month after it opens. Note that the ending cash balance line does not improve as quickly as it did in table 9.1. This means that although there is positive cash flow each month, it is not forecasted to be as much as in the previous scenario. In fact, this set of assumptions has the school generating a little less than $18,000 each month. This can be calculated by taking the ending cash balance for September and subtracting it from the same figure for October: $-130,489 - (-148,452) = 17,963$. There is a good possibility that a bank would fund the temporary cash shortfall in this scenario. The excess cash flow could pay off a loan in a relatively short time, probably about twelve to eighteen months, depending on the actual cash flow for the school.

In the worst-case scenario, the school starts out with a large deficit in the first month (no start-up grant), and just gets worse every month. Although this is not a likely scenario, it makes clear to everyone involved with the school that the start-up grant or something like it is essential and that the school needs to make sure to reach enrollment levels that will ensure the viability of the school. Clearly, the worst case could be somewhat improved by cutting expenses but probably not enough to ensure the school's survival.

Adjusting Forecasts

At this point in the planning process, the team should calculate additional scenarios to find out approximately what set of assumptions still make the school financially secure. It is highly unlikely that any outside funding source will support a school that projects monthly cash deficits every month, so a reasonable solution must be found to get the budget balanced and provide some level of reserves. This process is called a *"what-if" analysis*. The team should explore how far expenses could be reasonably cut to create a positive cash flow from the operation of the school, other possible sources of revenues, possible means to more effectively increase enrollments, other sources of grants, and creative ways to get by for less without sacrificing outcomes. With each idea, the management team should test the impact on the financial forecast spreadsheet. The specific nature of each what-if should be documented on the spreadsheet, and it is advisable to always begin each new what-if from the original integrated spreadsheet. Without such documentation, the process can get quite confusing. The what-if process systematically examines issues such as the following:

1. Are the enrollment estimates accurate? Any realistic efforts to improve enrollments should be explored. Some of these may have some costs that will need to be added to the expense forecast.
2. Are there granting agencies or foundations that would fund specific aspects of the school start-up, such as textbooks, library books, computers, software, staff development, scholarships, and so forth that have not been investigated?
3. At this point, the next iteration (the initial iterations were introduced in chapter 8) of the staffing plans should be developed. With the integrated financial statement, it is easier to specifically tie staffing what-ifs to enrollment levels. Staffing plans should investigate the effects of larger class sizes, fewer supervisors and administrators, fewer classroom aides, fewer educational support

staff, and fewer general support staff (such as clerical and maintenance).

4. Can benefit costs realistically be reduced? It may be possible to do so without significantly reducing the actual benefits. In addition, some benefits may not be essential during the start-up period. Insurance consultants or operating schools may be able to provide ideas for possible savings.

5. Can any equipment or furnishings expenditures be postponed? Is it possible to get by with less expensive options? Can used equipment meet the needs of the school? Have larger companies in the community been contacted about possible donations of furnishings and equipment?

As this list shows, it is best to spend time on items that can have the largest impact on the financial forecast.

A final part of the what-if process should include a careful examination of opportunities to use an entrepreneurial technique known as bootstrapping, which is finding creative ways to reach the same desired outcome while spending less. At the heart of successful bootstrapping is debunking a common myth about entrepreneurship. It often is assumed that a great deal of money is required to make a start-up really successful. In fact, many large, successful ventures started with very little money. These entrepreneurs found ways to make things happen and did not let limited funding deter their visions. The same can be true for educational entrepreneurs:

> It was very hard in the beginning for our school. We had no start-up funds at all in 1995. Because of the little money, we had to get creative about how to get our school funded. We began with trying to find grants. We received a couple of small grants, which helped in the planning stages of this school. To finance our facility, Community of Peace Academy became the first school in the state to use tax-exempt bonds for this purpose. When we finally opened, we had a 160 students and virtually no money. We had no computers and no library. We were buying kindergarten chairs at K-mart and dictionaries at Wal-Mart. Eventually, we gained more students and more funding, and within five years our budget had grown from a few thousand dollars to a couple million. We then decided to expand our school from a K–5, which it originally started out as,

to a K–12. (Dr. Karen Rusthoven, principal, Community of Peace Academy, Minneapolis, Minnesota)

There are a number of effective ways to bootstrap a new start-up. The following are some that apply to entrepreneurial school start-ups:

1. *Marketing:* Rely first on that which is free. Personal selling of the school to groups of prospective families by the management team is the most effective method of promoting the school. Local newspapers always are looking for community stories and are happy to work with new schools to write stories about their plans. It may be possible to get a website set up and hosted by a friend of the new school for free until the school gets up and going. This also is true with promotional brochures. Many of the ideas presented in chapter 6 are designed to be consistent with a bootstrapping approach to marketing the school.

2. *Staffing:* Schools can attract an incredible array of volunteers, many with high levels of talent. One new parochial school found parent volunteers who set up and operated all its computer networks. Parents and other volunteers can provide many of the administrative duties, facility repairs, and so forth, saving previous funds for teachers and educational staff. This is an important principle of bootstrapping: target spending on what is most important.

3. *Administrative overhead:* In addition to volunteer staffing, there are other methods of bootstrapping administrative aspects of the school. Used equipment is often more than adequate to meet the needs of the school. For example, one school was able to get a fairly sophisticated phone system donated by a local business that had outgrown their old equipment. The phone system was only two years old and included all the hardware the school could possibly use. The only cost was installation, and the school was saved over $5,000. While tools such as cell phones may be convenient, it is best to assign them only to those who need them for safety and security. Again, target spending only on what is truly essential for the education and safety of the children.

EXTERNAL FUNDING

Even with careful what-if analysis and bootstrapping, many schools still need to secure outside funding. In fact, every school receives one form of financing: credit from vendors. It is important to build a good personal relationship with all vendors and suppliers. That way, if cash flow is a little behind, it may be possible to postpone some payments until the cash comes in. However, ethically this should be done only with the full knowledge and consent of these businesses.

In addition to credit from vendors, schools may secure financing from banks and granting agencies. A financing plan should be developed that matches the needs of the school with the best source of funding:

> To raise capital for our newly proposed school, we did some bonding on the parts of the school building that were not used for religious purposes, such as the computer lab and library. We obtained capital in other ways, such as through grant writing and private donations. These forms of raising capital helped us start our school. (Mathew Metz, principal, St. Ambrose Catholic School, Woodbury, Minnesota)

Banks often are willing to fund short-term operating cash flow. For example, if a school is expecting large sums that will be coming in from a state agency or from a committed grant, the bank may be willing to lend money that will be repaid when these large payments come into the school. Banks may be willing to lend against accounts receivable, be it from public sources or private tuition payments owed to the school. Typically, a school can expect no more than about 70 to 80 percent of accounts receivables that are owed, and only more current balances are usually considered (under ninety days). Banks also can provide funding for equipment and furnishing (50 to 80 percent of original value), up-fit for facilities (50 to 70 percent of costs), and real estate (70 to 90 percent of value).

Leasing companies (some of which are part of larger banking companies) can lease a variety of equipment to a school, including kitchen appliances, office equipment, and furnishings. The advantage to leases is that the school does not need to fund part of the cost up front as is typically the case with a loan. Leases are particularly good for equipment that becomes obsolete quickly, such as computers.

If a school chooses to own its buildings rather than rent, real estate lenders are a source of such funding. Real estate lenders are an alternative to a traditional bank and may offer better terms, particularly if they have experience funding schools.

Corporations may be willing to become strategic partners with a school. Suppliers may be willing to pay fees for the right to become an exclusive vendor and to engage in some forms of promotion in the school. Public schools have participated in this type of arrangement with national soft drink companies and companies such as Channel One.

When pursuing funding from foundations and granting agencies, the single most common error is not understanding what these funders are willing to support. Some favor certain kinds of schools, such as charter schools. Others are only willing to fund certain types of expenditures, such as books or other tangible items.

There are other methods of funding a start-up school that are more in line with the theme of bootstrapping discussed earlier. For example, it may be possible to barter for something that is needed, such as offering to develop and produce marketing materials in exchange for reduced tuition. Some resources may be sharable and thus can be financed by others, including space for the school or even specialized staff.

Whatever source of funding is pursued, it is important to build an effective presentation. The heart of most presentations is a business plan or at least a summary of one. An effective presentation tells a story that is based on a compelling vision and that motivates the other party to want to support the school. An effective presentation is interactive. That is, it is important to listen to any feedback that is provided and not to try to make the potential funder commit resources at the initial meeting. If the funder is interested in supporting the school, the management team should understand that many of the terms in any documents may be negotiable. If necessary, it may be advisable to use the school's attorney or advisers as part of the negotiating process, as they are more experienced with such negotiations.

CREATING AND MANAGING THE BUDGET

Up to this point, the school has been working with multiple scenarios of the financial forecast. The budget that the school will use should be based on more conservative assumptions, such as those illustrated in table 9.2. The budget should be accompanied by a list of assumptions and the measurements that will be used to monitor them. The budget should be used as a guide and may need to be adjusted often during the first year of operation. If revenues are falling short of expectations, then budgeted expenses will need to be adjusted for subsequent months to offset this change. It needs to be stated again that a budget for a start-up school does not constitute permission for people to spend (as can be the case in public schools) but rather serves as a guide that will need to be carefully managed.

SUMMARY

This chapter, the last dealing with the development of the business plan, examines the process of creating integrated financial forecasts and budgets for a start-up school. Several adjustments may be required before the school has a sound, balanced budget. Specific aspects of the financing of a school may require outside funding, but the principles of bootstrapping are designed to help reduce this need. The rest of this book addresses the needs of a school as it begins to grow and develop. There are still many lessons that can be learned from successful entrepreneurs.

PART 3

The Start-Up and Beyond

CHAPTER 10

Building an Effective Culture

If the idea for the school makes it past the planning phase, then the challenges of the actual start-up begin. How well will the team implement the plan as it was developed? What changes will need to be made in the plan on the basis of new information or changing conditions? The start-up and early growth of a school is both exciting and stressful for all involved. The better prepared everyone is for what lies ahead, the better the chances are that the school will succeed. The business plan, examined in detail earlier in this book, provides a guide for the start-up and development of the new school. The rest of this book addresses the additional challenges that a school's leadership faces as it manages a growing organization. This chapter examines the process of developing an effective culture in a growing school. Chapter 11 discusses the role of leadership, building a successful team, designing effective systems, formulating marketing strategies, and managing succession.

CULTURE

Culture includes the shared beliefs about the organization's purpose and how its members should behave. The formation of a school's culture starts from the time the founders first come together to talk about starting a new school. The core values of these founders serve as the foundation of the school's culture (see chapter 2 for discussion of core values and their role in planning the school). Although the core values may be written, the real culture of a school cannot be represented in any manual.

In fact, culture is observed through the actions of its members. Culture defines how organizational members should act toward each other and how they should act toward external stakeholders. These actions can be understood through the organization's values, its norms, and, to some degree, its rules. Written descriptions of what an organization is "all about" may not reflect what is really going on. Written documents or oral descriptions of the learning environment of a school may have little in common with the manner in which the school operates on a day-to-day basis. Schools that stress the importance of respect in their written materials may actually demonstrate very little respect in how members act toward each other. What the organization values or considers important, what norms it enforces, and what rules it adheres to are what really shape the action of members.

The use of the word *members* in the definition of culture is intentional, as the culture defines who is really part of the organization. Different school cultures will define who is considered an insider, or member, in different ways. It is important to understand whom an organization defines as "we" and whom it defines as "they." Some schools take a very narrow definition of members, including only administrators, teachers, and other staff. These schools view students and parents as clients, outsiders, or stakeholders, not as true members. Other schools may draw a somewhat wider circle by also considering students as members. Yet other schools take an even wider view of members, extending their definition of membership to the wider local community. If the school leadership intends to have a more inclusive view of who truly is a part of the school, they must understand that membership in an organization goes well beyond mere rhetoric. It is not enough to simply state that parents and students are truly part of the school's culture. Culture is defined by how members act, not just by what they say. This is where the challenge lies in building a culture in a growing school. Actions matter, while rhetoric about values and beliefs do not.

The example from a junior high school discussed in chapter 6 illustrates the issue of culture. The school espouses that it is a community that includes staff, students, and parents. In orientations for new parents, the importance of parental involvement in the school is described as a fundamental aspect of what the school is all about.

Brochures emphasize that it is a school "fueled by parental volunteerism." But parents tell a different story. They say they are treated with indifference or even ignored by the staff when they arrive at the front office to report in for volunteer activities. They feel that many of the teachers show little gratitude for their help. What the principal describes as the school's culture and what in fact can be observed about the culture through the actions of its members are in stark contrast. It can't be emphasized enough that it is actions, not words on paper, that define culture.

Why do organizational cultures look so different? Simply stated, different founders bring a different set of values to each new school. In addition, groups of members that join these schools continue to shape these cultures over time. Administrators, teachers, board members, students, parents, and support staff move in and out of a school even during its first years of operation. Each can play a small part in shaping the culture as it evolves. Therefore, even though two schools are only a mile apart, they may have distinctly different cultures because of the various people who have passed through their doors. On the other hand, what is remarkable is how much most school cultures fundamentally have in common, even schools from different parts of the country. This is because members come from common professional bodies (teachers and administrators) and a common societal culture (American) that provide a common foundation for most school cultures.

Understanding how to build and develop a desired culture depends on the ability to assess what culture exists within a school. Aspects of a school's culture can be evident even as the doors open for the first day of classes. Assessing a culture is not an exact science but rather requires careful observation of a variety of factors. The following list can help guide the process of assessing and understanding an organization's culture:

1. *Observe "artifacts" of culture:* Artifacts are symbols of culture that can be found in members' everyday actions and in the physical work space itself. For example, students being seen moving freely in and out of teachers' offices throughout the day and parents being observed e-mailing teachers regularly to follow up on

classroom activities of their children tells much about the open-ness of the culture in that school. In the same school, teachers being seen moving in and out of each other's classrooms and ad-ministrators' offices for informal discussions throughout the day is further evidence of the openness that exists within the culture of that school.

Now imagine a second school where students attend classes regularly but do not meet or talk with teachers outside of class. Teachers keep to themselves, never venturing from their own classrooms. These actions would be artifacts that indicate a rather impersonal and closed culture within the school.

An example of physical space as an artifact of culture might in-clude the presence or absence of displays showing the character of the school and the accomplishments of its students. Elaborate displays that clearly show widespread student and staff involve-ment might be artifacts that indicate a culture in which members are highly committed and proud of their membership.

2. *Rituals and ceremonies:* Rituals and ceremonies can demonstrate what the organization considers important. For example, most schools have ceremonies to recognize student success in academ-ics and various extracurricular activities. However, the level of participation in the ritual or ceremony helps one understand the true value placed on the focus of the recognition by the culture. If students, teachers, and parents attend ceremonies to recognize ac-ademic achievement in large numbers, it shows that academic achievement is truly valued in the culture of the school.

3. *Decision making:* Both the process of making decisions and the locus of decision making help one understand an organization's culture. Who makes major decisions? Who provides input into the decisions? Is the process of decision making open? How ef-fective is the follow-through on decisions that have been made? These are the types of questions that can help one understand the culture of decision making in the organization.

4. *Affect:* The types and strength of the emotions of the members of the organization are a key part of culture. Emotions can indicate the degree of commitment to the culture. Members may react passion-ately to any attempt to change the culture. Strong positive feelings

toward the school and even a sense of fun associated with work can lead to more effective outcomes. Members will react most passionately and enthusiastically to those things that are most valued in the culture of the organization.

5. *Stories:* Stories are told within any organization. Often these stories communicate messages or morals that are part of the organization's culture. In fact, stories have been a tool for teaching within cultures for thousands of years. Stories that are told time and again, especially those told to newcomers to the organization, help paint a picture of what rules, values, and norms are important. Stories will often be told about people who did not fit in or about major blunders that violated stated or unstated norms of behavior. These stories play the role of providing a clear warning of what is expected to become a "full member" of the culture. For example, the message of a story could be that loners are not tolerated or that high performance is expected from everyone. These stories can be powerful tools to shape the behavior of new members.

6. *Heroes:* Culture can also be reflected in which people are chosen to be "heroes." While some stories are told to warn newcomers what not to do, heroes are created by a culture to personify the best of what it values. In a school, it may be a teacher or a staff member whose actions went way beyond expectations to support that which the organization values most. For example, the hero may be a teacher who puts in dozens of extra hours to help a student who is on the brink of getting off track. On the other hand, if a teacher who "cheats" the system or finds creative ways to "get by" were a hero, this would certainly be a clear indication of a dangerously negative culture. Those people the organizational members consider to be heroes should be closely examined, as this will give a clear window into the school's culture.

7. *Ethics:* An important function of culture is to communicate what is considered right and wrong. Some ethical standards are written down in ethical codes, while others are unwritten norms that are learned over time. All the ethical standards, both those written and those understood through tradition, help define the core values of the organizational culture.

Assessing an organization's culture is not a quantifiable exercise, to say the least. It requires patient observation and an open mind. Through qualitative, unbiased assessment of the issues listed here, a picture of an organization's culture should start to emerge.

Since everyone who comes into the school shapes its culture, it is quite possible that this culture may at some point no longer reflect the intentions of the original founders. If this occurs, the leadership of the school can deliberately change its culture to more closely reflect the core values of its founders. For example, the founders of a private mental health system that included state-licensed schools began to realize that through the growth of this organization, the culture had fundamentally changed. Said one of the founders, "We no longer recognized the business we had started only a few years before." They decided that they needed to do whatever they could to restore the original culture of this organization and reinstate the core values that they used to guide its formation and early development.

Changing culture takes time, and it can be quite difficult to implement. Changing culture requires deliberate, consistent, and patient actions. Clearly, culture cannot simply be changed by issuing a new directive or by setting up training sessions. One cannot order employees to change their values and beliefs through a memo or e-mail. However, even many larger business organizations have been able to change their cultures.

Changing culture requires a clear and honest understanding of where the culture is now. A thorough assessment of the current culture is the critical first step in changing culture. It is also important to understand how the culture evolved to become the way it is. This includes getting to "know the ghosts" of past administrators and informal leaders who helped shape the culture. Changing culture also requires a very clear vision of what the changed culture should ultimately look like.

Success in changing to a more entrepreneurial culture requires the development of a comprehensive plan. This plan should not be a written plan that sits in a drawer or gathers dust on a shelf; rather, it should be a commitment to action. A plan for cultural change should include the following elements:

- *Leadership:* The leadership of the school should have a relentless focus on the vision of where the school should be headed and what culture is needed to get there. Leaders should provide inspiration for the school and be clear on their view of its potential. Leaders must also be prepared to serve as "emotional shock absorbers" for the distress caused by change. Even the most enthusiastic employees can become disheartened at times and lose focus. The leadership must remain outwardly positive and committed, especially when things get really tough. Leaders must maintain this outward confidence even during periods when they are experiencing their own doubts. They create clear objectives and milestones to help members assess progress. Finally, they lead by example to set ethical standards and expectations.

- *Communication:* The leadership should provide consistent and frequent communication about the vision of where the organization is headed and what the culture must become to get there. In fact, this vision should be woven into all significant communications. Successful agents of organizational change never miss an opportunity to remind employees of where the organization is going. They always find a way to talk about the vision when answering questions and issuing new policies. The vision should be communicated to new and prospective employees during recruitment and orientation. A statement of the vision should be displayed prominently, even hung on the wall. It should be integrated into handbooks and personnel manuals and talked about in all organizational communications.

- *Rewards:* Rewards can either foster or suppress culture and its change. Even though schools typically cannot use large bonuses or raises as rewards, they do have many options that can be powerful. For example, administrators can utilize a portion of their discretionary expenditures, such as money to pay for conference attendance, to reward those who embody the desired culture. Evaluation criteria for promotions and merit pay can also be expanded to include behaviors that reflect the desired cultural change. And never underestimate the power of public recognition. Awards can be created to recognize those who best exemplify the traditions that represent the founding culture. Over time, an effective reward system will help attract those who share the values representing the founding culture and help retain those who never have strayed from that vision.

- *Criteria for recruitment:* Many organizations wait too long to address one of the more important means of changing culture: recruitment. Most school systems have clearly defined systems for recruitment. Recruitment systems usually include specific criteria to evaluate new hires. These criteria evolve as the culture changes. If the organization continues to bring in new members who fit the undesired emergent culture, change will not occur. To help the process of changing culture, selection criteria should be modified to increase the number of employees who fit in with the desired culture.
- *Structure:* Changing structure to more closely resemble the desired culture also will help the process of change. Structure helps shape how staff members interact with each other, and how staff interact helps define the norms and values and will support the process of changing culture.

Changing culture requires deliberate action and will take time. Many schools fail to take the time and effort necessary to truly change the culture of their organization when it gets off track. There is no one single change or intervention that will change organizational culture. This requires attention to a variety of factors and can consume much of a leader's time.

SUMMARY

Culture defines what a school is all about. A school's culture begins to form even before the school opens its doors for the first day of classes, being formed by the core values of its founders. Over time, the culture can change and at some point may no longer reflect the intentions of its founders. While changing culture to bring it in line with its origins is possible, it takes time and deliberate actions on the part of all the members of the organization. The next chapter examines issues associated with effectively managing the growth of the school.

CHAPTER 11

Managing Growth

Entrepreneurs who succeed in navigating the ups and downs of starting a new school soon realize that some of the biggest challenges come not with getting the school going but with keeping it going as it grows. As many new businesses fail during the growth phase as fail during start-up. Managing growth requires strong leadership that keeps everyone involved with the school focused on the vision. Management must work to develop effective systems that can accommodate the needs of the growing complexity in the school. The school must be able to continue to attract the right staff, including teachers, support staff, and management. The leadership must be ready to adapt to change, particularly in their marketing plans. Finally, the school must, almost from its beginnings, start to plan for the eventual succession of the founders and the leadership team.

LEADERSHIP

Many of those who get involved in new school start-ups do so because they love education or are passionate about educational reform. Such passion is not unlike what is seen among any group of entrepreneurs. Many entrepreneurs have never run a start-up enterprise before. In fact, studies have found that only half of entrepreneurs have ever been entrepreneurs of other ventures of their own or worked with other entrepreneurs in their start-ups. This percentage seems to be even higher among educational entrepreneurs. Therefore, for many of these entrepreneurs, each stage of the organization's development is a new experience and leads to an evolution in the entrepreneur's role and responsibility. This transition can be frustrating for many, as it is their passion for education that drew them into the start-up to begin with. As the school grows, the leader may find him- or herself less and less involved with what drew him or her to the start-up in the first place: a passion for education. Administrative requirements grow and take up an increasing percentage of the leader's time. And if the organization gets large enough, the leader will face the challenges of organizing those responsibilities among a growing management team.

Arguably, the single most important aspect of an entrepreneurial leader's role in a growing organization is the effective use of the vision that the founding team forged for the school. The founders' core values are a fundamental part of this vision. Therefore, the vision for the school will play a major role in developing its culture as the staff grows. Communication of the vision helps to ensure that all its members become a part of its culture. Entrepreneurs have found a variety of effective means to communicate vision. The vision often is placed prominently in company handbooks and personnel manuals. Sometimes it is proudly displayed as a plaque on the wall. The vision can be talked about consistently in company communications, such as newsletters and websites. New members of the school also must learn about the vision, so it should be integrated as an important part of employee orientation. The founding entrepreneur should be able to present the vision and history of the school to new employees to underscore the importance of these traditions.

Vision should be used as a criterion to choose management team members as the school grows. New leaders must share the vision, as they must help put it into action. If they do not, the type of dysfunctional change in culture discussed in the previous chapter can incrementally start to take place. In summary, a key role of the entrepreneurial educator is to create a shared vision that lasts well beyond the first day of classes, throughout the growth and evolution of the school.

A clear vision is critical during the changes that arise because of growth. Vision helps define what is fundamentally important. As one entrepreneur described it, "Sometimes it gets hard to remember you're here to drain the swamp [vision] when you're up to your ears in alligators [stresses caused by growth]." A clear vision provides clarity and focus for employees and provides a context for decision making. Entrepreneurs and the type of managers whom they tend to attract can come up with many innovative ideas for new projects. A focused vision can help ensure that only those ideas that are consistent with the intentions for the new school are seriously considered. It can provide discipline to a group that is, by nature, rather undisciplined.

Some have described a second role that leaders of growing organizations take on as therapeutic or even pastoral. Growth and change can create significant uncertainty and distress among staff. The leader should take on the job of an emotional shock absorber during stressful times. One entrepreneur tells the story of a particularly stressful time in his business. Cash flow was not keeping up with growth, and the entrepreneur was seriously concerned about the future of the company. One day he was feeling depressed about the state of his venture. He did little that day to hide his concerns. As he tells the story, he walked to his office with his head held low, barely acknowledging his employees. As he sat down at this desk, a woman who had been with him from the very first day of the business stormed into his office. "Don't you ever drag yourself in here that way again!" she demanded. "We look for you to tell us how things are going, and if you come in looking that way, we all lose hope." He took her words to heart and recognized that if his employees did not believe the business could survive, it most likely would not survive.

EFFECTIVE SYSTEMS IN A GROWING SCHOOL

A growing organization has the need for systems that keep pace with its growing complexity. During the start-up, there is little time for developing systems. The team is busy defining their vision, recruiting families, and trying to secure all the resources they will need to operate the school (money, facilities, staff, and so forth). As the school grows, the leadership needs to transition from such entrepreneurial activities to those more consistent with a professionally managed organization. That is, it becomes increasingly important to develop the systems that will be needed to sustain the school as it grows. Planning, administrative, financial, and communication systems all need to be implemented or improved.

Planning Systems

Entrepreneurs mistakenly assume that the planning function ends with the completion of the business plan. In fact, planning needs to become a part of how the organization is managed. Planning should not be a one-time or even annual event. The logic of the business plan as discussed in this book must become a part of every manager's job and a part of every action taken. The outcomes of planning should be evident in every decision and every communication within the team. Although an annual planning retreat is a common ritual in many organizations, it may not be necessary if everyone on the team embraces the discipline of effective planning. Put simply, planning is deciding what needs to be done, how it is going to be achieved, and how its outcomes will be measured and assessed. Even the most elaborate business plan really addresses only these three factors.

Administrative Systems

A common description for administrative systems is the "plumbing" of an organization. Administrative systems ensure that cash flows in and out in a timely manner, that supplies arrive on time, that personnel records are in place, and that students get enrolled. As a school gets larger, it may need to put in place more sophisticated accounting systems. Such systems are required to create the type of data needed for effective decision making. Billing and collections for student accounts will see a system of simply sending invoices replaced by one that focuses on reducing days in accounts receivable to increase cash for growth. Human resource systems will need to include not only written policies and job descriptions but also salary guidelines, consistent promotional strategies for openings, legal compliance, and compensation planning. If food services are managed in-house, systems will need to ensure increasing efficiency and effectiveness to keep costs from getting out of control and maintain quality at expected standards.

Financial Systems

Initially, most start-up ventures rely on financial control systems based on budgets and statements that reflect historical compliance with the budgeted figures. In other words, they manage where they are going based on data reflecting where they have been. In a static world, this does not cause too many problems, as the future looks much like the past. But in the world of a growing school, each month can bring new challenges that cannot be understood simply by looking at the past. A business professor uses an interesting exercise to illustrate the problems with relying only on historical data. He takes his students into an empty parking lot. In the middle of the lot is a series of orange cones and a car. The object is for the students to navigate the course set up by the cones. There is, however, one catch to the exercise. The car has all the windows blacked out with paper except for the rear window. The students must navigate the cones driving forward but are able to look only backward through the rearview mirror. The car careens all over the lot, rarely making it past even the first cone. The lesson is clear to all: It is impossible to really know where you are headed while looking only at where you have been.

A residential school for behaviorally troubled children had open admissions throughout the year. As the school began to grow, it became more difficult to predict census in the coming weeks and months. This led to ineffective staffing and uneven cash flow. The administrator decided to develop a method of financial reporting that could provide a better forecast of admissions (and thus census) rather than continuing to rely on the monthly financial statements he received from his accountant. His team examined the steps in getting a child admitted to their program. The first step was an inquiry in which general information was shared about a child who might be referred (if the contact person was not familiar with the facility, that information was provided). If the child appeared to be a possible candidate for admission, a formal referral would, it was hoped, follow. The child and his records would then be evaluated for possible clinical acceptance. If the child was clinically accepted, it was then ascertained whether the family or other sources of funding had the financial ability to pay for the recommended period of stay in the facility. If funding was available, the child was set up for admission. Generally, the entire process took from four to eight weeks. Figure 11.1 displays this process.

For the first time, this model allowed the school to predict admissions with some accuracy. For every thirty contacts made in one

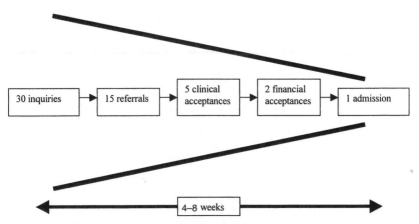

Figure 11.1. Admissions Process for a Residential School

month, they could expect one admission about one or two months in the future. So if they had ninety contacts in January, they could expect three admissions sometime between February and March. But this was just one benefit of this new reporting system. The team began to examine several of the ratios in the model and ask important questions. Why did they lose half the children between inquiry and referral? The answer was simple. They found that staff did not return calls promptly and that referrals were lost to other facilities. Why were two-thirds of the referrals clinically denied? The answer was that the staff members were being too conservative about admissions, not recognizing the importance of their reviews for the growth of the facility. The number of financial denials led the team to decide to invest in hiring a new salesperson who could establish contracts with more funding sources, such as county agencies and insurance companies. The 50 percent conversion from acceptance to admission was found to be a function mainly of time; that is, the process simply took too long. Therefore, attention was aimed at ways to streamline the process, leading to significant improvement. The overall ratio from inquiries to admissions dropped in half, and the time decreased to an average of two weeks. Every organization has processes like this example that help show where the business is headed and that can be easily understood and measured to create better financial control.

Communication Systems

During the start-up period for a school, most communication flows through the entrepreneur. As the organization grows, several changes need to take place in communication:

- Communication must flow freely throughout organization and not be expected to pass through the entrepreneur. Instead, it should flow from those who have the information directly to those who need it.
- The most effective communication is that which is open and honest.
- Both formal and informal communication systems will be required. Although the use of e-mail and other, more formal communication increases in a growing organization, the informal network should not be discounted or suppressed, and everyday face-to-face contact should never be abandoned.
- Communication includes effective feedback.
- Information should be viewed as a shared resource, not one to be hoarded for the sake of power or influence.
- Technology should be a tool to enhance communication, but different schools will have different needs.

THE TEAM REVISITED

The importance of a building an effective team does not end at start-up. Some of the initial team members will not successfully grow personally and professionally as the school grows. New team members will need to be promoted or hired to replace these individuals. Other new team leaders will need to be hired to fill emerging gaps in the management needs of the school. If effectively selected, new members can help bring stability, order, and structure to the growing school. These new members can bring in new solutions to old problems and can broaden the team's perspective for decision making.

Changing needs of the organization will require changing roles of the original management team. Ongoing management assessment and organizational needs assessment should be conducted to help create development plans for the training and education of team members. Changing organizational needs also will create a continuing need to attract the best talent available. As discussed in chapter 7, networking and searching for good talent from other schools are excellent ways to find new team members. The culture, the quality of the team, and the flexibility that an entrepreneurially run organization can offer can help attract that talent to the school's management.

MARKETING AS THE SCHOOL GROWS

Marketing should be thought of as a process, not an event. That is, marketing should not be relegated to the summer months as thoughts shift to the upcoming year. Marketing activities should occur throughout the year, and it should be understood that almost everything that goes on in the school is part of the marketing function. The "product" of the school is defined and redefined through each child's experience in the school and through every contact people have with the school and its employees. Promotion occurs with every public event and article written about the school. It occurs with every staff member representing the school by attending a conference. The value of pricing is defined by the reputation for quality that is built up over the months and years that the school is in operation. It is essential to stress to all staff that they are part of the marketing process of the school in everything they do. Their successes in marketing the school should be celebrated, recognized, and rewarded. Even seemingly minor contributions can work together to create marketing success.

The processes learned while performing the feasibility analysis and market research should continue in the operating school. The very events and conditions that created the opportunity for the school are likely to change, at some point requiring the school to change in minor or even significant ways. Data about the industry and competitive environment, society, and public policy should be gathered systematically. This information will give the management team the tools it needs to identify and formulate strategies to adapt to an ever-changing environment. This is the key to keeping the entrepreneurial spirit alive within the school.

MANAGING SUCCESSION

At some point, every entrepreneur leaves the organization he or she founded. In a school, this includes the founding management team and the founding board. Even the types of consultants and advisers the school needs may change along with the school itself. Ideally, the transition process may begin with thought and discussion during the business planning process.

Certain consultants and advisers are best suited for start-up or smaller organizations. Many of these advisers recognize their limitations and actively work with the management team to plan for a transition. Likewise, some board members plan from the very beginning to have a limited term. The management team should respect the wishes of these board members and take full advantage of what they can offer the school while on the board.

The reasons for management succession are many. Some founders are entrepreneurs who revel in the start-up. When the school gets to a more static state, these individuals may become restless and need to pursue other more entrepreneurial endeavors. Some of the founding team may find that they no longer have a clear role in the organization as it gets larger. For others, it may just be time to retire or at least slow down a bit. For all members of the team, they should ask two important questions: Am I staying too long? and Am I leaving too soon?

Succession is best managed with a clear transition plan. Such a plan should identify time frames and milestones that may trigger the succession process to begin. Plans should be in place either to develop current members of the management team so that they can move up the organization or to identify candidates from the outside to be recruited. If the plan is to develop an insider, training, education, and experiential opportunities should be set up to provide the skills and knowledge required. Under no circumstances should anyone be promised such a promotion. Not all transition plans progress as originally formulated. It may take several attempts to discover the right path to a successful succession.

The founder should be thinking about important postsuccession issues. The entrepreneurial experience can be all-consuming, and many entrepreneurs spend little or no time thinking about what succession will mean to them personally. There is a phenomenon from real estate known as "seller's remorse," which entrepreneurs can experience even if they do not actually own the school they helped found. Even without formally owning the school, such as in the case of the founders of a nonprofit, it still is emotionally *their* school. After they leave the school, they may begin to have second thoughts about their decision. In some cases, the entrepreneur may actually try to take back their old position, which normally ends poorly for all concerned. Long before the succession takes place, the entrepreneur should develop a life plan that lays out what will happen to him or her personally after leaving the school. Experienced entrepreneurs recommend that a person take time before entering any new venture and to remember the aspirations that brought the entrepreneur into the new school from its inception.

SUMMARY

This book has presented a model to help new schools learn from the lessons of successful entrepreneurs. From the initial vision to the feasibility assessment to the business plan and through the growth and development of the school, the educational entrepreneur faces successes and false starts, highs and lows, and triumphs and trials. But for most, the entrepreneurial experience is one that is worth it all.

References

Bagley, C., and C. Dauchy. 1998. *The entrepreneur's guide to business law.* New York: West.

Bhide, A. 1992. "Bootstrap finance: The art of start-ups." *Harvard Business Review*, November–December, 109–17.

Bielick, S., and K. Chandler. 2001. Homeschooling in the United States: 1999. NCES 2001-033. Washington, D.C.: U.S. Department of Education.

Blechman, B., and J. Levinson. 1991. *Guerrilla financing.* Boston: Houghton Mifflin.

Brown, R., and J. Cornwall. 2000. *The entrepreneurial educator.* Lanham, Md.: Scarecrow Press.

Caggiano, C., and J. Finegan. 1995. "Bootstrapping: Great companies started with less than a thousand dollars." *Inc.*, August 1.

Clark, T. 2001. "Virtual schools: Trends and issues." Unpublished manuscript commissioned by Distance Learning Resource Network and WestEd Project.

Cornwall, J., and N. Carter. 2000. "University of St. Thomas entrepreneurial self-assessment." St. Paul, Minn.: John M. Morrison Center for Entrepreneurship, University of St. Thomas.

Cornwall, J., and M. Naughton. 2003. "Who is the good entrepreneur? An exploration within the Catholic social tradition." *Journal of Business Ethics*, 61–75.

Cornwall, J., and B. Perlman. 1990. *Organizational entrepreneurship.* Homewood, Ill.: Irwin.

Cornwall, J., D. Vang, and J. Hartman. 2004. *Entrepreneurial financial management.* Englewood Cliffs, N.J.: Prentice Hall.

Flamholtz, E., and Y. Randle. 2000. *Growing pains.* San Francisco: Jossey-Bass.

Godin, S. 1998. *The bootstrapper's bible.* Chicago: Upstart Publishing.

Levinson, J., and S. Godin. 1994. *The guerrilla marketing handbook.* Boston: Houghton Mifflin.

Winborg, J., and H. Landstom. 1997. "Financial bootstrapping in small businesses—A resource-based view on small business finance." In *Frontiers of entrepreneurship research,* ed. P. D. Reynolds et al. Babson, Mass.: Babson Center for Entrepreneurial Studies, 471–85.

http://nces.ed.gov/programs/coe/2002/section1/tables/t02_3.asp

http://nces.ed.gov/pubs2002/digest2001/ch2.asp

www.csus.edu/ier/charter/bizpl.html

www.edreform.com/pubs/chglance.html

Index

About the Author

Jeffrey R. Cornwall holds the Jack C. Massey Chair in Entrepreneurship at Belmont University in Nashville, Tennessee. Previously, he was the Sandra Schulze Chair in Entrepreneurship at the University of St. Thomas in St. Paul, Minnesota. He was cofounder, president, and chief executive officer of Atlantic Behavioral Health Systems, which provided a full continuum of mental health programs and included state-licensed private schools. Cornwall writes extensively on entrepreneurship and consults regularly with a variety of for-profit and nonprofit organizations, including charter schools and other educational organizations. He has coauthored three other books, including *The Entrepreneurial Educator.* Cornwall also taught at the University of Wisconsin–Oshkosh and the University of Kentucky.